Deutsch konkret

A German Course for Young People

Workbook 1
Chapters 1–10

Peter Boaks, Ebba-Maria Dudde

LANGENSCHEIDT

BERLIN · MUNICH · VIENNA · ZURICH · NEW YORK

Deutsch konkret
A German Course for Young People

Workbook 1

by
Peter Boaks and Ebba-Maria Dudde

in co-operation with
Christine Dunbar and the "Deutsch konkret" team:
Gerd Neuner, Peter Desmarets, Hermann Funk, Michael Krüger and Theo Scherling
Volker Leitzbach (photography)
Drawings and layout: Theo Scherling

Cover design: Bjarne Geiges and Theo Scherling
Editorial work: Manfred Glück

Printed in Germany · ISBN 3-468-96746-2

10 9 8 7 6 * 92 91 90 89 88

Contents

Why learn German?   5

Unit 1   10

Unit 2   25
Landeskunde 2   38

Unit 3   39
Landeskunde 3   48

Unit 4   49
Landeskunde 4   61

Unit 5   63

Revision, Units 1 - 4   66

Unit 6   73
Landeskunde 6   83

Unit 7   85
Landeskunde 7   94

Unit 8   95
Landeskunde 8   104

Unit 9   105
Landeskunde 9   114

Unit 10   115

Revision, Units 6 - 9   119

Landeskunde 10   126

Focus on Grammar   129

Why learn German?

It's useful!

It's important!

It's fun!

How can it be useful?

- For holidays in German-speaking countries. Every travel agent can offer holidays in Germany, Austria or Switzerland - summer holidays or winter sports. Look through the brochures - you will see famous cities, beautiful countryside, rivers, lakes and mountains.

- For working in these countries. Many do - engineers, skilled workers, businessmen, teachers, students, servicemen and their families and many other people too.

- For making friends in these countries. The best way to do this is through exchanges. This means that you stay with a German, Austrian or Swiss family and a boy or girl from that family then stays with you. Many schools have exchanges and towns and boroughs are also "twinned" with places in these countries.

- You do not even have to go abroad! For many jobs in this country it is useful to know German. There has been a great increase in trade and business of all sorts with German-speaking countries - And don't forget: their young people and tourists come here too!

Can y o u think of other ways in which it would help to know German?

Why is German important?

We should try to understand people from other countries and to get on with them. An enormous number of people in Europe speak German.

Look at the diagram below. The figures, in millions, show roughly how many people use that language as their mother tongue - that means the language they speak at home, at school or at work.

Who speaks German?

You should not think that each language is limited to one country only. German is spoken not only in West Germany and East Germany but also in Austria and Switzerland as well as in some parts of France, Italy, Luxemburg, Poland, Czechoslovakia, Rumania and Russia. Can you find out exactly which languages are spoken in the countries of Europe? Make a list. (Remember that we are talking about the "mother tongue" and not about foreign languages studied at school).

The languages of Europe

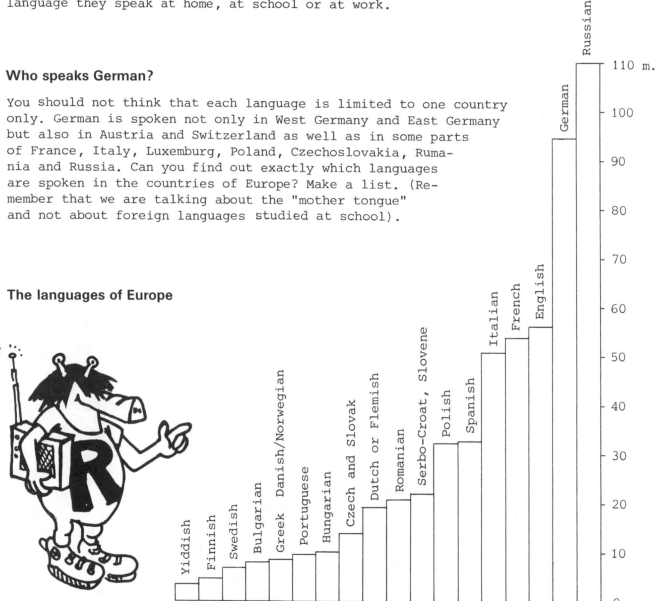

Learning German is fun – and easier than you think!

A good way to learn is to stay for a while in the foreign country - if possible with a family on an exchange programme. You could also write to a pen-friend in one of these countries.

However, if you cannot do this yet, you should still be able to learn a lot of German quite quickly. There is a good reason for this - many German words do not look or sound so different from English.

Why are German and English so similar?

Most European languages have grown up over the centuries as a large and widely spread family. Within this family of languages German and English are very closely related. Dutch and Flemish, Danish, Norwegian and Swedish are also very close. Did you know that Old English is also called Anglo-Saxon? Can you find out who the Angles and the Saxons were and where they came from? Here are some common German words. Can you guess what they are in English?

Relatives

Mutter _____

Vater _____

Sohn _____

Tochter _____

Bruder _____

Schwester _____

Everyday things

Haus _____

Wagen _____

Stuhl _____

Schuh _____

Buch _____

Licht _____

Food and Drink

Wasser _____

Bier _____

Brot _____

Fleisch _____

Apfel _____

Animals

Katze _____

Schwein _____

Kuh _____

Maus _____

Schaf _____

Now try this too.

You can probably fill in the details of your name, address, etc.

Familienname: _____

Vorname(n): _____

Adresse: _____

Schule: _____

Klasse: _____

(Of course some of these words are simply borrowed!!)

We think that you will enjoy learning German and that you will have great fun if you can visit these countries and meet people, young and old.

When you do meet them, you will understand them and they will understand you.

Viel Spaß!

Here is a list of useful addresses:

Council of Ministers of Education
Canada 252
Ministry of Education
Bloor Street W.
5-200 Toronto/Ontario M5S 1V5

German National Tourist Offices:
London, Montreal, New York, Washington

The Central Bureau for Educational
Visits and Exchanges
Seymour Mews House, Seymour Mews
LONDON W1
Council on International Educational
Exchange (CIEE)
205 E. 42nd St.
NEW YORK NY 10017

Organise exchanges and visits for
young people

German Tourist Facilities Ltd.
184 Kensington Church Street
LONDON W8
Cheap travel to and from Germany

Youth Hostel Association
14 Southampton Street
LONDON WC2

American Youth Hostels Inc.
132 Spring Street
NEW YORK NY 10012

Canadian Hostelling Association
333 River Road
Vanier City/Ontario K1L 8B9

What do these pictures tell us about Germany?

Deich an der Nordsee ▲

◄ Auf einem See im Voralpenland

◄ Schwarzwald

Hamburg ►►

Die Alpen ►

Im Ruhrgebiet ▲

Der Rhein ►

Klasse 7a, Goethe-Schule

Ü1 Bitte ausfüllen

Please fill in what they are saying.

Remember: They don't have to be saying exactly the same things as in the textbook.

Try to do it without looking it up -
but if you cannot remember you can look at the textbook.

Ü2 **Dialoge üben und schreiben**

Try these conversations with the person sitting next to you.
Write them up later.

Hallo, ich heiße **Uwe** . – Und wie heißt du?

Dreizehn.

Ich bin **Martin** . Ich bin **vierzehn.** Wie alt bist du?

1. Susanne 13			Katja 14
2. Eva 12			Peter 13
3. Christian Meier, 16			Emine Tamm, 14
4. Carola Schulz 11			Christine Huber (auch) 11
5. Sonja Weber 13			Stefan 12

Ü3 Wer ist das?

Ask these questions:

1. Wie heißt er/sie?
2. Wo wohnt .....? (in ...)
   Woher kommt .....? (aus ...)
3. Wie alt ist .....?

1.

Das ist mein Lehrer.

Wie heißt er?

Hans Bieler
Kassel

Now ask Karl and Susanne about their friends.

2.

Freundin

Monika

14

Kassel

Wer ist das?
Das ist _____

3.

Freund

Andreas

13

Helsa

Wer ist das?
Das ist _____

Ü4 **Wie heißt Nr. .....? Woher kommt er?**

A German football team

① Karl-Heinz Rummenigge, München

② Harald Schumacher, Köln

③ Manfred Kaltz, Hamburg

④ Hans-Peter Briegel,
   Kaiserslautern

⑤ Horst Hrubesch, Hamburg

⑥ Paul Breitner, München

⑦ Bernd Förster, Stuttgart

⑧ Wolfgang Dremmler, München

⑨ Klaus Fischer, Köln

⑩ Pierre Littbarski, Köln

⑪ Karl-Heinz Förster, Stuttgart

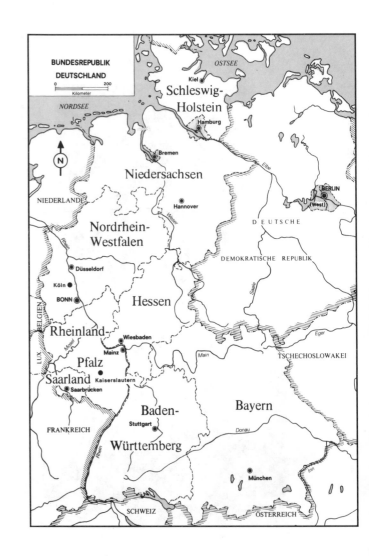

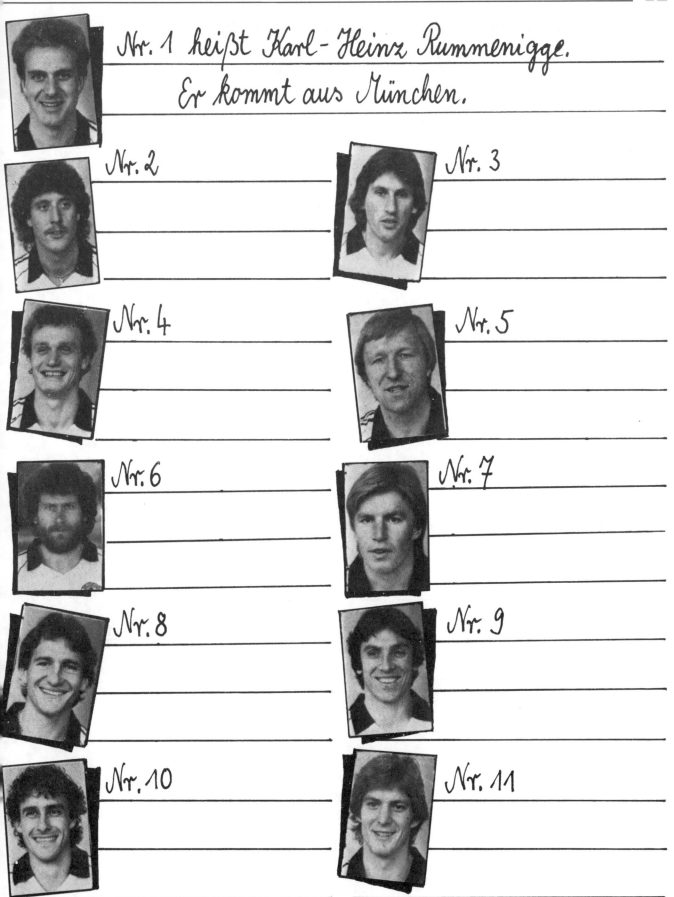

Nr. 1 heißt Karl-Heinz Rummenigge.
Er kommt aus München.

Nr. 2

Nr. 3

Nr. 4

Nr. 5

Nr. 6

Nr. 7

Nr. 8

Nr. 9

Nr. 10

Nr. 11

Can you find out the names of some German football clubs or the names of Germans
who are famous in other sports?

Ü5 **Bitte einsetzen: heißen/kommen/sein/wohnen** *Can you fill in the gaps?*

1. Hallo, Freunde, ich _**heiße**_ Karl. Ich _____ in Bremen. Meine

   Freundin _____ Sabine. Sie _____ zwölf und ich _____

   dreizehn.

2. Guten Tag, ich _____ Emine und _____ aus Kassel. Meine Lehrerin

   _____ Karin Steger. Das _____ Karl. Er _____ mein Freund.

   Er _____ vierzehn.

3. Guten Tag. Ich _____ Bieler und _____ Lehrer. Meine Schule

   _____ in Kassel. Ich _____ aus Frankfurt.

4. Karl und Emine _____ Freunde. Sie _____ in Kassel.

5. Karin Steger und Hans Bieler _____ Lehrer. Frau Steger _____ aus

   Helsa. Herr Bieler _____ in Kassel.

Ü6 **Bitte Fragen schreiben** *Can you write the questions to go with these answers?*

**Woher kommst du?** _____ Ich komme <u>aus Kassel</u>.

_____ 1. Ich heiße <u>Christine</u>.

_____ 2. Andreas und Ute sind <u>aus Berlin</u>.

_____ 3. Mein Freund heißt <u>Peter Schulz</u>.

_____ 4. Ich bin <u>vierzehn</u>.

_____ 5. Das ist <u>Frau Müller</u>.

_____ 6. Carola wohnt <u>in Köln</u>.

_____ 7. Uwe ist <u>dreizehn</u>.

_____ 8. Ich bin <u>Sonja Weber</u> und

   komme <u>aus Bonn</u>.

Ü7 **Rechnen auf deutsch** *Can you do these sums in German?*

3+8?   *Wieviel ist drei plus acht?*   – *Elf.*   11

7+9? _____ – _____ 16

14–1? _____ – _____ 13

2·6? _____ – _____ 12

18:3? _____ – _____ 6

15–5? _____ – _____ 10

4·5? _____ – _____ 20

11–8? _____ – _____ 3

16:4? _____ – _____ 4

17+2? _____ – _____ 19

Ü8 **Bitte das ganze Wort schreiben** *Write out the words in full.*

Liebe Maria,   17.6.

Das i①t meine Sc②le. Sie heißt
Goethe-Schule. I③ ④n in Klasse
7a. D⑤ Klassenlehre⑥ heißt Karin
Steger. Mein Le⑦er heißt Hans
Bieler. Meine Freu⑧in heißt Astrid.
⑨e ist vierzehn. Mei⑩ Freun⑪
Klaus ist dreizehn und wo⑫t in
Kassel. Meine Freunde in K⑬sse 7a
wohn⑭ in Kassel. Frau Steger
kom⑮ aus Helsa.

Deine Monika

① ☐☐☐☐☐ ② ☐☐☐☐☐☐☐

③ ☐☐☐☐ ④ ☐☐☐☐

⑤ ☐☐☐☐ ⑥ ☐☐☐☐☐☐

⑦ ☐☐☐☐☐

⑧ ☐☐☐☐☐☐

⑨ ☐☐☐

⑩ ☐☐☐☐☐ ⑪ ☐☐☐☐☐

⑫ ☐☐☐☐☐

⑬ ☐☐☐☐ ⑭ ☐☐☐☐☐

⑮ ☐☐☐☐☐

Ü9 Internationale Wörter schreiben

Many words are international. Can you match the words below with the pictures?

1. Fußball
2. _____
3. _____
4. _____

5. _____
6. _____
7. _____
8. _____

9. _____
10. _____
11. _____
12. _____

13. _____
14. _____
15. _____
16. _____
17. _____

Motor   Kilo   Tourist   Film   Scheck   Fußball   Antenne
Omnibus   Gitarre   Cassette   Reisepaß
Caravan   Clown   Telefon   Hamburger   Cola   Information

Ü10 **Englische Wörter im Deutschen** *Many English words are used in German ...*

Look out for others too.

Ü11 **Bitte die Beispiele ansehen** *Look at these examples*

der Ball   das Telefon   die Gitarre

mein Ball!   dein Ball?   mein Telefon!   dein Telefon?   meine Gitarre!   deine Gitarre?

Mein!   oder   Dein?

mine!   *or*   *yours?*

M_____ Hamburger!

D_____ Kamera?

D_____ Cassette?

M_____ Buch!

Ü12 **Bitte ausfüllen**

Can you fill in the missing words and endings?

1. Das ist Christof.

   _____ ist dreizehn.

   _____ wohn_____ in München.

2.

> Hallo, ___ heiß__ Eva.
> ___ wohn__ in Bonn.

3. Hier ist Sonja.

   _____ komm_____ aus Hamburg.

4. Das sind Katja und Stefan.

   Wie alt _____ _____?

   Wo wohn_____ _____?

5. Und du?

   Wie heiß_____ _____?

   Wie alt _____ _____?

   Wo wohn_____ _____?

Ü13 **Fünf deutsche Wörter schreiben**

*Make a list of 5 German words (not names of people or towns)
which start with a capital letter even when they come in the
middle of a sentence.*

_____ _____ _____ _____ _____

What kind of words are they? _____

Ü14 **Zahlen** *Numbers*

Wie viele? *How many? Give your answer in words.*

_____

_____

_____

Und wie viele sind kaputt?

_____

Ü15 **Bilder von Sportlern sammeln**

Collect some pictures of famous athletes from your country. Choose three of them and say who they are and where they come from.

Ü16 *Wer bin ich?*

a) *Introducing yourself*

I_____ h_____ _____ .
                                          (name)

I_____ _____ _____ , und i_____ w_____ ____ _____ .
                  (age)   (hometown)

Meine S_____ _____ _____ .
          (school)   (name of school)

I_____ _____ in Kl_____ _____ .
                                        (year)

*Now give this information about yourself to the rest of the class or to your
neighbour.*

Wer ist das?

b) *Imagine that this is a photo of a friend.
Try to introduce him or her.*

Das ist mein(e) _____ .

_____ (his/her name)

_____ (his/her age)

_____ (where he/she comes from)

c) *If you met a young person from Germany, Austria or Switzerland, what questions would you ask? (name? age? where ... from?)*

1. _____?

2. _____?

3. _____?

d) *Now choose a picture of someone in your family, your circle of friends or out of a magazine.*

What questions would your classmate ask you to find out who this is?
Try to write 4 questions.

1. _____

2. _____

3. _____

4. _____

Now write out the full conversation in your exercise book.

e) ## Und wer ist das?

Das sind Mary und Peter.

Sie _____ dreizehn.

Sie _____ aus Schottland

und _____ in London.

Ü1 **Dialoge schreiben** *Complete these conversations. Practise them with a partner.*

① Ist das Herr Siegert?

Wer ist das?

Heißen Sie ...?

Ich weiß nicht.

Guten Tag!

Entschuldigung!

Sind Sie ...?

② Nein, das bin ich nicht. Mein Name ist Braun.

Ich weiß nicht.

_____?

_____.?

③ _____?

_____.?

Ja, ich komme aus Hannover.

Ja, ich heiße Vogel.

Kommen Sie aus ...?

Freut mich.
Und wer sind Sie?

Wo wohnt ...?

Ich heiße ...

Nein, das ist er nicht!

④ Wie heißen Sie bitte?

Mein Name ist Schulz.

_____

_____?

_____

Ü2 **Dialoge schreiben** *What are they saying?*

Ü3 Wieviel kostet das in deinem Land?

Explain to a German visitor roughly how much things cost for him.

a) *Give approximate prices in your currency and then convert the prices into Marks for him. You can check the exchange rate at a bank or in the newspaper. For example:*

Eine Cola kostet ... - das sind achtzig Pfennig.

Ein Popkonzert-Programm kostet ... - das sind vier Mark.

Ein Hamburger kostet _____

Ein Mineralwasser kostet _____

Eine C90-Cassette kostet _____

Eine Gitarre kostet _____

Eine Kamera kostet _____

Eine Postkarte kostet _____

Ein Radiorekorder kostet _____

DEVISEN- UND SORTENKURSE

15. 11.

Währung	Devisen (amtl. Kurse)		Sorten (im Freihdl.)	
	Geld	Brief	Ank.	Verk.
USA (1 $)	2.6734	2.6814	2.62	2.72
England (1 £)	3.965	3.979	3.91	4.06
Canada (1 c$)	2.1615	2.1695	2.11	2.21
Holland (100 hfl)	89.18	89.40	88.–	90.–
Schweiz (100 sfr)	123.70	123.90	122.25	125.25
Belgien (100 bfr)	4.916	4.936	4.75	5.–
Frankreich (100 FF)	32.79	32.95	31.75	33.75
Dänemark (100 dkr)	27.73	27.85	26.50	28.50
Norwegen (100 nkr)	35.90	36.02	34.75	36.50
Schweden (100 skr)**	33.81	33.97	32.75	34.50
Italien (1000 Lire)**	1.647	1.657	1.61	1.71
Österreich (100 öS)	14.187	14.227	14.10	14.34
Spanien (100 Ptas)**	1.730	1.740	1.64	1.78
Portugal (100 Esc)**	2.10	2.12	1.50	2.30
Japan (100 Yen)	1.1405	1.1435	1.10	1.16
Jugosl. (100 Din)**	–	–	1.50	2.30
Griechenl. (100 Dr.)**	–	–	2.20	3.–
Türkei (100 Ltq)**	–	–	0.70	1.40
Finnland (100 Fmk)	46.65	46.85	45.25	47.25
Irland (1 lr. £)	3.109	3.123	3.–	3.15
100 Ostmark = Westm. Ankauf 19.– Verkauf 22.–				

b) **Bitte diesen Dialog üben**

Practise this short conversation with a partner.

o Was kostet das?

● Drei Mark fünfzig.

o Wieviel ist das in £ / $?

● _____

Herzliche Grüße aus dem Urlaub!

Ü4   Karten schreiben *Writing postcards*

Use some of these phrases. The textbook will give you some more ideas if necessary.

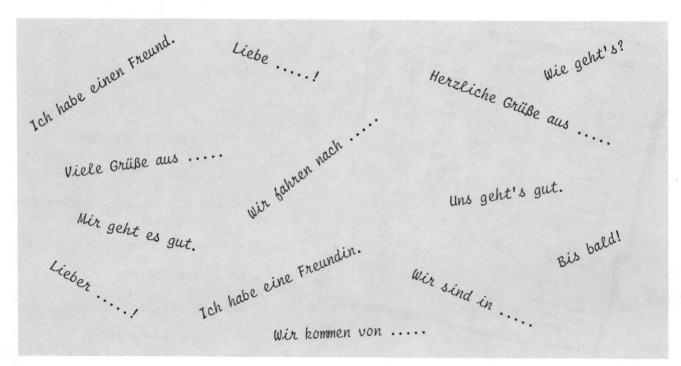

Ich habe einen Freund.   Liebe .....!   Wie geht's?

Herzliche Grüße aus .....

Viele Grüße aus .....   Wir fahren nach .....

Uns geht's gut.

Mir geht es gut.

Lieber .....!   Ich habe eine Freundin.   Wir sind in .....   Bis bald!

Wir kommen von .....

Ü5 Bitte ausfüllen

Complete this account of the Neumann family on vacation using the words below.

Beate aus Salzburg

Horst und Max

Familie Neumann macht Urlaub

Das _____ Familie Neumann. Herr _____

ist Ingenieur. _____ Neumann ist Sekretärin.

Kurt ist 14, seine Schwester Inge zwölf. Sie

_____ in Offenbach bei Frankfurt. Familie

Neumann _____ einen Caravan. Im Urlaub

fahren _____ oft an die Nordsee. Diesmal

_____ sie auf einem Campingplatz bei Wilhelms-

haven. Kurt und Inge haben _____ Zelt, Herr

und Frau Neumann schlafen im Caravan.

Auf dem Campingplatz gibt es _____ junge

Leute. Da ist Beate Neupert aus Salzburg _____

Österreich. Sie ist 14. Hans Zeller _____

aus Genf. George Schumacher _____ in Straß-

burg. Das ist in Frankreich.

Die meisten jungen Leute _____ aus

Norddeutschland. Grete, 13, ist aus Bremen.

Andreas, 12, ist aus Bielefeld. Horst und

Max kommen _____ Wuppertal.

wohnt   sind   sie sind   Neumann ist   kommt   hat   Frau ein
viele   wohnen   in   aus

Ü6   Mit dem Katalog einkaufen

Shopping from a catalogue

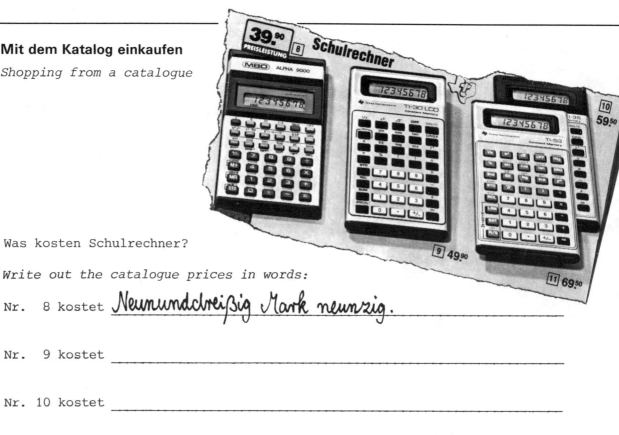

Was kosten Schulrechner?

Write out the catalogue prices in words:

Nr. 8 kostet *Neununddreißig Mark neunzig.*

Nr. 9 kostet _____

Nr. 10 kostet _____

Nr. 11 kostet _____

Ü7   Moon-Boots für den Winter

Karl needs a new pair of winter boots. He takes size 42 and has only DM 40 to spend.
Suzanne has DM 60 to spend. She takes size 36 and would like a pair in beige.
Which pair do Karl and Suzanne choose and how much do they pay?
Remember - the price varies according to size. Check the small print!

10 Garantiert warme Füße habt Ihr in diesem Moon-Boot aus Nylon. In Blau/Rot. Mit PVC-Schalensohle. Herausnehmbarer Moltopren-Innenschuh.
Bestell-Nummer 773 017

Gr. 1 (24,25,26), Gr. 2 (27,28)	29,90
Gr. 3 (29,30), Gr. 4 (31,32)	34,90
Gr. 5 (33,34), Gr. 6 (35,36) Gr. 7 (37,38), Gr. 8 (39,40) Gr. 9 (41,42)	39,90

11 Gegen Wind und Wetter geschützt in diesem Moon-Boot aus PU-Material. In Blau/Rot. Toll ist die 2farbige, profilierte PVC-Sohle. Innenschuh aus Moltopren, herausnehmbar.

773 028	Gr. 23, 24, 25	45,90
	Gr. 26, 27, 28, 29, 30	47,90
773 174	Gr. 31, 32, 33, 34, 35	49,90
	Gr. 36, 37, 38, 39, 40	55,90

12 Wenn's so richtig kalt wird, ist der gerade richtig: Moon-Boot aus Nylon in Beige/Blau/Rot. Der Innenschuh ist herausnehm- und waschbar. Rutschsichere PVC-Profilsohle.
Bestell-Nummer 743 730

Gr. 1 (31,32), Gr. 2 (33,34)	49,90
Gr. 3 (35,36), Gr. 4 (37,38) Gr. 5 (39,40)	55,90

	Moon-Boots			
	Order Number	Size	Colour	Cost
Karl				
Suzanne				

Ü8 **Swinging Monos with a Great Sound**

	Sanwa 5007 199,-	Rio 7016 99,50	Contec 2012 129,50	Sanwa 7024 199,-	Sanwa 2042 75,--
radio					
alarm					
headphone socket					
2 loudspeakers					
built-in microphone					
operates with batteries					

Which is the best buy? Mark the functions offered with these cassette recorders.

5 Radio-Recorder SANWA 5007, mit eingebauter 24-Stunden-Uhr. So werden Sie immer pünktlich durch Summton oder Musik geweckt. Für UKW- und MW-Empfang. Eingebautes Mikrofon. Anschlüsse für Kopfhörer und TA-Kristall. Pausentaste. Batteriebetrieb mit 4 x Typ UM 2. Gehäuse: braun/goldfarbig, mit versenkbarem Griff und Teleskopantenne. B/T/H: 30/9/18 cm.
Bestell-Nummer 712 726
199,-

6 Preiswerter Mono-Radio-Recorder Rio 7016, für UKW- und MW-Empfang. Mit eingebautem Mikrofon. Batteriebetrieb mit 4 x Typ UM-2. Gehäuse: grau. Maße (B/T/H): 28/10/17 cm.
Bestell-Nummer 712 635
99,50

7 3-Band-Radio-Recorder CONTEC 2012 für UKW-, KW- und MW-Empfang. Eingebautes Mikrofon. Anschluß für Kopfhörer. Batteriebetrieb mit 6 x Typ UM 2. Gehäuse: silberfarbig. Mit Tragegriff und Teleskopantenne. Maße (B/T/H): 30/9/20 cm.
Bestell-Nummer 712 356
129,50

8 Spitzen-Radio-Recorder SANWA 7024. 6 Watt und 2 Lautsprecher-Systeme. Für UKW-, KW-, MW-, LW-Empfang. Eingebautes Mikrofon. Anschlußbuchsen für Kopfhörer. Pausentaste. Bandzählwerk mit Nullstelltaste. Batteriebetrieb mit 6 x Typ UM-1. Gehäusefarbe: anthrazitmetallic, mit Griff und Teleskopantenne. Maße (B/T/H): 37/11/24 cm.
Bestell-Nummer 710 226
199,-

9 Preiswerter Automatik-Recorder SANWA 2042 für Netz- und Batteriebetrieb. TB und Radio. Eingebautes Mikrofon. Batteriebetrieb mit 4 x Typ UM-2. Gehäuse: braun, mit Tragegriff. Maße (B/T/H): 15/26/6 cm.
Bestell-Nummer 716 385
75,-

Flotte Monos mit vollem Sound

● Mit Weckeinrichtung
● Mit Einschlaf-Automatik

5 SANWA 199,-

6 99,50

7 129,50 3 Wellenbereiche

6 6 WATT MUSIK LEISTUNG

LED-Schaltuhr

8 199,- Preissenkung ● 2 Lautsprecher ● Einschlaf-Automatik

9 75,-

Ü9 **Bitte ausfüllen** *Can you complete what these people are saying?*

Ich bin Rocky.

Das ist _____ Bruder Roxy.

Und das ist _____ Schwester Rockine.

Rocko und Rocka heißen _____ Eltern.

my...

Wir sind Uwe und Sabine.

Und das ist _____ Bruder Karl.

our...

Wir heißen Uwe und Martin.

Das ist _____ Freund

und _____ Freundin

aus Holland.

HENK   MIEKE

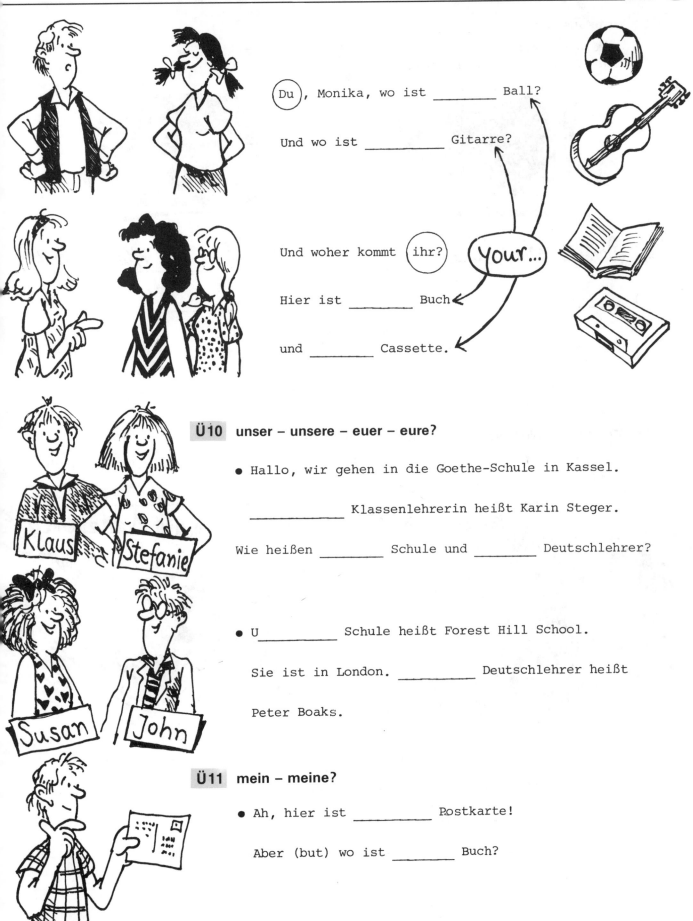

(Du), Monika, wo ist _____ Ball?

Und wo ist _____ Gitarre?

Und woher kommt (ihr?)   *your...*

Hier ist _____ Buch

und _____ Cassette.

Ü10   **unser – unsere – euer – eure?**

● Hallo, wir gehen in die Goethe-Schule in Kassel.

_____ Klassenlehrerin heißt Karin Steger.

Wie heißen _____ Schule und _____ Deutschlehrer?

● U_____ Schule heißt Forest Hill School.

Sie ist in London. _____ Deutschlehrer heißt

Peter Boaks.

Ü11   **mein – meine?**

● Ah, hier ist _____ Postkarte!

Aber (but) wo ist _____ Buch?

33

2C

Ü12 **Bitte ausfüllen**

Here are a number of objects. Show whose they are.
The clues are in the brackets.

(ich) *Das ist meine Cassette.*   (ich) *Das ist* _____ *Hamburger.*

(ihr) _____   (ihr) _____

(wir) _____   (wir) _____

(du) _____   (du) _____

Ü13 **Wer? Wie? Wo? Woher? – Fragen und antworten**

Now look at these pictures. Then write questions and answers with the words suggested above.

Wer seid ihr?

Wir heißen Max und Moritz. Und ihr?

_____   _____

_____   _____

_____   _____

_____   _____

_____   _____

34

Ü14 Fragen und Antworten schreiben

Write questions and answers.

① Ist das dein Freund ?

Ja, das ist

Ü15 **Dialoge ergänzen**

Can you complete these conversations?
Read them through first.

a) o Guten Tag! Ich bin Martin.

   • Hallo, Martin.

   o Und wie _____ ____?

   • _____ _____ Bill.

     Woher _____ ____?

   o Aus Hamburg.

     Und wo _____ ____?

   • In Cardiff.

b) o Wer _____ _____?

   • Das ist Monika.

   o Wie _____ _____ _____?

   • Dreizehn. _____ _____ in Kassel.

   o Und das ist Klaus?

   • Ja, das _____ _____.

c) o Entschuldigung, _____ _____ Herr Schulz?

   • Ja, und _____ _____ _____?

   o Supermann ist mein Name.

   • Woher _____ ____?

   o _____ _____ vom Krypton.

   • Wo _____ _____?

   o Da oben!

d) o Woher _____ _____?   o _____ _____ vierzehn.

 • Wir _____ England.   _____ _____ aus ...

 o Und wie _____ _____?

 • _____ _____ Debbie

 und John.

 o Wie _____ _____ _____?

 • _____ _____ zwölf und

 dreizehn. - Und ihr?

Ü16 Bitte fragen

Try to produce questions to match the following answers.

o Heißt du Uwe?   • Ja, ich heiße Uwe.

o _____?   • Ja, mein Name ist Bieler.

o _____?   • Nein, ich wohne in Kassel.

o _____?   • Nein, das ist Frau Steger.

o _____?   • Ja, er kommt aus England.

o _____?   • Nein, wir sind aus Dänemark.

Ü17 Wörter und Wendungen

Words and phrases.

 Two friends meet after some time. What would they say to each other?

a) o Hallo, _____ _____?

 • _____, _____.

 You want to know who someone is, but your friend doesn't know.

b) o W_____ _____ _____?

 • I_____ _____ _____.

Ü18 Try to write your own conversation(s) or work with a friend.

Will I ever go there?

Millions of visitors from Britain, Canada and the USA go to the German-speaking countries every year. Here are some figures:

Total number of visitors from the U.K. to: The Federal Republic of		the USA	Canada
Germany (F.R.G.)	1,116,000	1,349,000	115,700
Austria	377,000	535,365	56,446
Switzerland	418,000	2,071,855*	197,857*

*hotel overnights

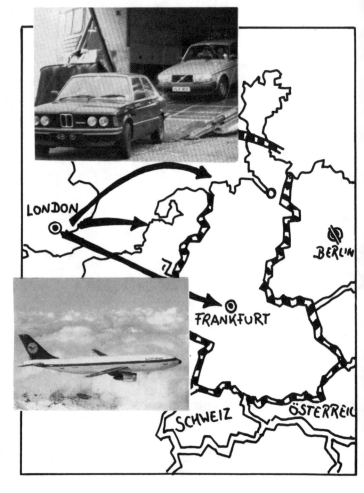

What was the purpose of each visit – why did they go?

As tourists on holiday:

F.R.G.	343,000
Austria	328,000
Switzerland	268,000

On business:

F.R.G.	407,000
Austria	24,000
Switzerland	92,000

To visit friends and relatives:

F.R.G.	280,000
Austria	19,000
Switzerland	45,000

Other reasons:

F.R.G.	86,000
Austria	6,000
Switzerland	13,000

During the same period a total of 1,855,000 German-speaking visitors came to Britain.

Now can you answer these questions?

1. *Did we visit Germany more often as tourists or as businessmen/women?*

2. *Why might so many people in this country have relatives and friends in Germany?*

3. *Why are Austria and Switzerland so popular with tourists?*

4. *Why would there be so many business trips to Germany?*

Ü1 Vorstellen

These young people from lesson 3 are telling us about themselves. What would they say?

Now <u>you</u> say who they are and where they come from.

Ich heiße Mbawi Kano und bin aus Nigeria.

Mbawi Kano ist aus Nigeria.

Wir heißen Bente Juul und Hanne Jensen und kommen aus Dänemark.

Bente Juul und Hanne Jensen kommen aus Dänemark.

①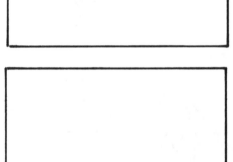

②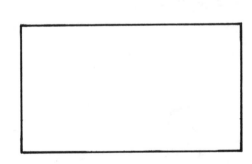

③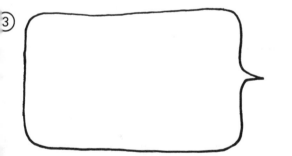

④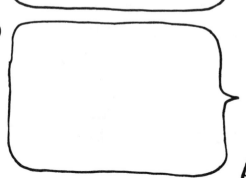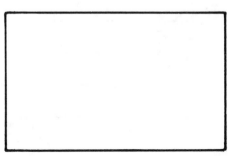

Ü2 **Dialoge üben und schreiben**

Practise these conversations with a partner and then write them up afterwards.
The first one is done for you.

> Wie heißt du? / Woher kommst du? / Wo liegt das? /
>
> Wie heißen Sie? / Woher kommen Sie?

Ich heiße Akira Kôyô
     – und wie heißt du?   Ich heiße Hanne Jensen.
                                   Woher kommst du?

            Aus Osaka.

                   Und wo liegt das?

In Japan. Woher kommst du?

                   Aus Odense.

        Wo liegt das?

                 In Dänemark.

Ü3 Eine Ansichtskarte beschreiben

Describing a postcard

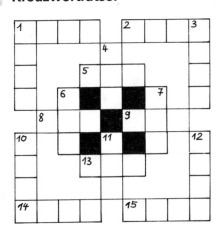

Christine sends Reiner a postcard from London and explains to him what can be seen:

Oben links, das ist das Parlament.

_____

_____

_____

Ü4 Kreuzworträtsel

1 → Wie alt ... du?
1 ↓ "Deutsch konkret" ist ein ...
2 → Wir ... aus Japan.
3 ↓ Zahl
4 ↓ Wer ist ...?
5 → Guten ...!
6 ↓ ... heißt Eva.
7 ↓ Das ist ... Buch.
8 → Ich ... ein Schüler.
9 → ... kommen aus Italien.
10 ↓ Das ist ... Buch.
11 ↓ Ich bin ... Tokio.
12 ↓ ... ist aus Buxtehude.
13 → ...en Tag!
14 → ... ist nicht Ja!
15 → ... liegt am Rhein.

Was schreibt Reiner?

Can you find out and write in English what Reiner has told Christine about Munich?

Ü6 Was ist das hier? Wie sagt man auf deutsch? *What are these things in German?*

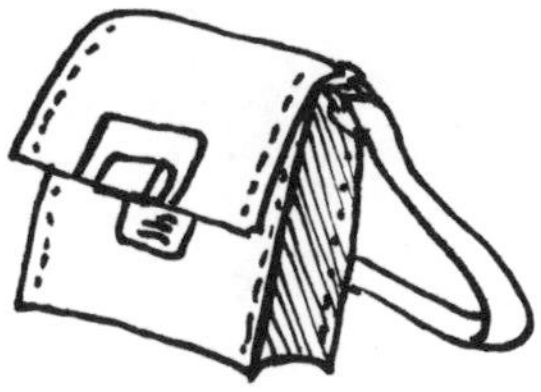

E _____ _____   e _____ _____   e _____ _____

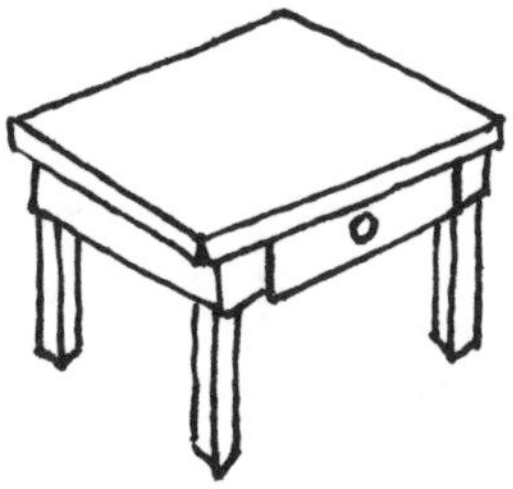

e _____ _____   e _____ _____   e _____ _____

ein? eine?

_____ Schule, _____ Tafel, _____ Lehrer, _____ Buch,

_____ Freundin, _____ Fußball, _____ Cassette

Ü7

der Ball ist rund   *die Tafel ist breit*   *das Buch ist neu*

Collect more d e r, d i e, d a s *words. Make sure you put them into the right baskets.*

der   *die*   *das*

der, die, das?

_____ Landkarte, _____ Heft, _____ Stuhl, _____ Geld, _____ Jugendherberge,

_____ Tisch, _____ Freund, _____ Klasse, _____ Gitarre, _____ Herr,

_____ Nummer, _____ Kugelschreiber

Ü8 Schreibe Pluralformen

Siebenunddreißig Jungen _____ _____

_____ _____

_____ _____

_____ _____

_____ _____

Ü9 Im Klassenzimmer

What objects are there in your classroom? How many of each? Make a list.

Beispiel: 20 Tische   das Bild, -er   das Fenster, -   die Tür, -en

Ü10 **Formen von** *sein* **und** *haben*

Use correct forms of sein *and* haben.

Ich bin 13 und habe 2 Schwestern.

Er _____ 4 und _____ 5 Fußbälle.

Sie _____ 10 und _____ 20 Platten.

Es _____ 20 und _____ viel Spaß. (fun)

Wir _____ 14 und _____ 30 Cassetten.

Sie _____ 16 und _____ 6 Freunde.

haben *Ask questions.*

_____ du 50 Pfg.? — Nein, leider nicht.

_____ ihr 5 Mark? — Ja, hier bitte.

_____ Sie 2 Groschen? — Moment, ich weiß nicht.

Ü11 Bitte buchstabieren

What are these words in German?
Write them down and spell them out to your
neighbour afterwards.

country _____   live _____

youth hostel _____   how/what _____

write _____   where from _____

Ü12 Bitte ausfüllen *Fill in this identity card.*

Personalien

Schul-
stempel

Name: _____

Vorname: _____

Geburtsdatum: _____

Wohnort: _____

Straße, Nr.: _____

Ort und Tag der Ausstellung:

_____ , den _____ 19 ____

Schul-
stempel   _____

(Unterschrift des zuständigen Lehrers)

Foto

_____

(Unterschrift des Inhabers)

Ü13 Fragen stellen *Asking questions.*

a) *How would you change these questions if you were talking to more than*
   one person?

1. Wie heißt du? _____

2. Wo wohnst du? _____

3. Wie alt bist du? _____

4. Wie heißen Sie? _____

5. Woher kommen Sie? _____

What would you ask,

1. *if you wanted to know what something is called in German?*

_____

2. *if you did not understand what someone was saying?*

_____

3. *if you did not know where a certain place is?*

_____

Ü14 **Länder in Europa**

Write the German names of countries 1 - 9.

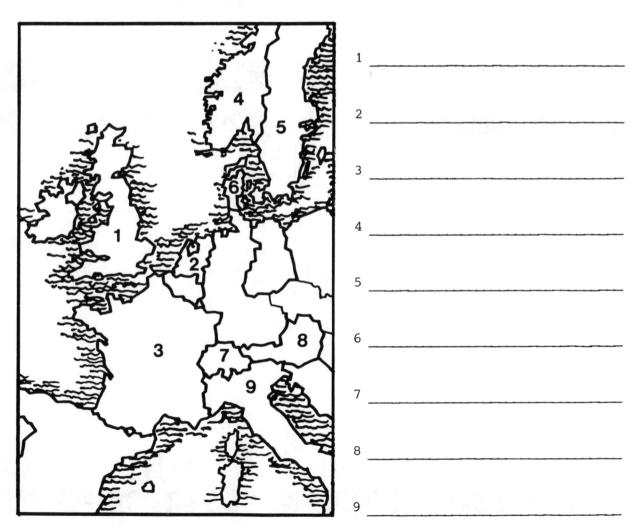

1 _____

2 _____

3 _____

4 _____

5 _____

6 _____

7 _____

8 _____

9 _____

BURG SCHWANECK

Jugendherberge u. Jugendbildungsstätte Burg Schwaneck

There are 563 youth hostels in Germany.
The address of the central office is: Deutsches Jugendherbergswerk,
Bülowstr. 26, 4930 Detmold 1

Kurzinformationen über alle Jugendherbergen

Postleitzahl	Jugendherberge / Adresse / Herbergseltern	Lvb	Telefon	Betten	Tagesräume	Hobby- u. Sporträume	Warmwasser	Dusche	Familienzimmer	Kochgelegenheit	Vollverpflegung	B	Freibad	Hallenbad	Wintersport	ev. Kirche	kath. Kirche	Bahnhof	Bus	Straßenbahn	Besondere Bedingungen	Seite
5100	**Aachen „Colynshof"** Maria-Theresia-Allee 260 Waltraud und Helmut Banäcker	Rheinl.	0241 71101	178	6	—	x	x	—	x	—		10	10	x	x	x	20	5	—	* ⊙ ●	S. 258
7080	**Aalen** Schubert-Jugendherberge Stadionweg 8 Anneliese u. Manfred Moravec	Schwab.	07361 49203	104	4	1	x	x	2	x	—		10	—	x	x	x	25	5	—	⊙	S. 301
2243	**Albersdorf/Holstein** Bahnhofstraße 19 Sabine u. Rainer Götz	Nordm.	04835 642	84	2	2	x	x	5	x	—		30	45	—	x	x	5	—	—	⊙	S. 234
7297	**Alpirsbach** Reinerzauersteige 80 Rita und Wolfgang Kilp	Schwab.	07444 2477	150	5	—	x	x	—	x	—		40	5	x	x	x	10	—	—	* ⊙	S. 301

This excerpt from the German Youth Hostel Handbook tells you all you need to know about the hostels. Can you understand what the pictures are telling us? The key below will help.

Key to symbols:

- Postleitzahl
- Jugendherberge / Adresse / Herbergseltern
- Lvb
- Telefon
- Betten
- Tagesräume
- Hobby- und Sporträume
- Warmwasser
- Dusche
- Familienzimmer
- Kochgelegenheit
- Vollverpflegung
- für Behinderte geeignet s. Seite 25/26
- Freibad
- Hallenbad — Minuten
- Wintersport-Möglichkeiten
- ev. Kirche
- kath. Kirche
- Bahnhof — Minuten
- Bus — Minuten
- Straßenbahn
- Besondere Bedingungen
- mehr über die JH / Seite

Ü1 **Schulfächer** *School Subjects*

Bitte ausfüllen

a) *Find the subjects which fit these gaps - remember you go down the columns.*
   Bettina's timetable in the course book will help you if necessary.

```
  1   2   3   4   5   6   7
  H                   
  A               
  N               
  D   E   U   T   S   C   H
  A               
  R               
  B               
  E               
  I               
  T               
```

b) *Now you have found the subjects
   - what do you think of them?*

Deutsch *macht Spaß!*

_____

_____

_____

_____

_____

_____

..... { macht Spaß!
       ist Spitze!
       ist Klasse!
       ist interessant!

..... { macht keinen Spaß!
       ist langweilig!
       ist doof!
       ist nicht interessant!

Ü2 **Interview mit Bettina**

What answers would Bettina give to these questions?
(Check the details in the course book.)

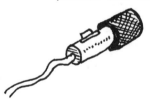

Hast du Montag Kunst?

Bettina: _____

Und Sport ist Freitag?

Bettina: _____

Hast du auch Biologie?

Bettina: _____

Wann hast du Mathe?

Bettina: _____

Ist das interessant?

Bettina: _____

Und Englisch?

Bettina: _____

Und wie findest du Deutsch?

Bettina: _____

Danke, Bettina.

Ü3 **Vergleiche deinen Stundenplan mit Bettinas Stundenplan:**

Compare your own school timetable with Bettina's. Do you take the same subjects?
If so, for how many lessons per week? Find out the German for any other subjects
you take.

	Bettina			Ich	
Ja/Nein + −	Stunden			Ja/Nein + −	Stunden
+	5	Deutsch			
		Mathematik			
		Englisch			
		Physik			
		Biologie			
		Chemie			
		Geschichte			
		Erdkunde			
		Sozialkunde			
		Handarbeit			
		Kunst			
		Musik			
		Religion			
		Sport			

Now write full sentences about some subjects which you both do.

For example: Bettina hat 5 Stunden Deutsch. Ich habe _____ Stunden Deutsch.

Bettina _____

Ich _____

Ü4 **Brieffreunde** *Pen-friends*

The pupils in Bettina's class were asked to write a short letter introducing themselves and their school to a class from a school in this country, hoping that some pupils might write back and become pen-friends. Being lazy they decided on a standard form which everyone could use, merely filling in their own details from their timetables.

Fill this one in for Bettina and then write a similar sort of letter in German about yourself.

Lieber Brieffreund! (Liebe Brieffreundin!)

Mein Name ist _____ . Ich bin _____ .

Ich wohne in _____ und gehe in Klasse _____ .

Mein Klassenlehrer / Meine Klassenlehrerin heißt _____

_____ . Am _____ habe

ich _____ . Das ist _____ !

Am _____ habe ich _____ .

Das ist _____ und macht _____ .

Wie ist es bei Dir in der Schule?

Schreib bald!

Mit herzlichen Grüßen   _____

Now write a letter about yourself and your school.

_____ !

_____

_____

_____

_____

Ü5 **Was sagt der Lehrer?** *What might the teacher be saying?*

Ü6 **Was sagen die Schüler?** *What might the pupils be saying?*

Ü7 Schreibe dein eigenes Zeugnis!

Write your own school report!

Remember the German system of grades from 1 to 6. These drawings will help you:

1 sehr gut

2 gut

3 befriedigend

4 ausreichend

5 mangelhaft

6 ungenügend

Zeugnis

für

_____   _____   _____
(Vorname)   (Name)   (Klasse)

Religion   2   _____   ____

Englisch   ____   _____   ____

_____ ____ _____ ____

_____ ____ _____ ____

_____ ____ _____ ____

_____ ____ _____ ____

Bemerkungen: _____

_____

Ü8 **Stundenpläne**

Karin and Hans attend different kinds of schools. Can you see how their timetabl[es]
differ?
Which school has lessons in the afternoon?
Which type of school offers more practical subjects?
How many lessons of German do Karin and Hans have?
Which type of school offers more languages?

Hauptschule Feldbergstrasse — Karin Berg, 7 A

	Montag	Dienstag	Mittwoch	Donnerstag	Freitag	Samstag
8⁰⁰– 8⁴⁵	Physik/Kunst	Deutsch	Deutsch	Deutsch	Deutsch	
8⁴⁵–9³⁰	"	Mathe/Englisch	Mathe/Englisch	Mathe/Englisch	"	
9³⁰–10¹⁵	Deutsch	Geschichte	"	Geschichte	Mathe	
10⁴⁰–11²⁵	Mathe	Geographie	Religion	Religion	Mathe	
11²⁵–12⁴⁰	Sport	Physik/Kunst	Physik/Textil. Arbeit/Mathe	Englisch	Englisch	
12²⁰–13⁰⁵	"	"	Werken	Arbeitslehre/Musik	Biologie	

Physik/Kunst are
taught in groups

	Montag	Dienstag	Mittwoch	Donnerstag	Freitag	Samstag
7⁵⁵– 8⁴⁰	Mathematik	Deutsch	Religion	Kunst	Englisch	
8⁴⁰–9²⁵	Deutsch	Geschichte	Französisch/Latein	"	Sport	
9²⁵–10¹⁰	Englisch	Französisch/Latein	"	Biologie	"	
10³⁵–11²⁰	Französisch/Latein	Englisch	Englisch	Deutsch	Französisch/Latein	
11²⁰–12⁰⁵	Geschichte	Geographie	Musik	Mathematik	Mathematik	
12⁰⁵–12⁵⁵	Religion	Mathematik	Biologie	"	Musik	
13⁵⁵–14⁴⁰		Turnen	Turnen			
14⁴⁰–15²⁵		(Jungen) "	(Mädchen) "			

Dieser Stundenplan gehört: *Hans Klein, Klasse 7 B, Holbein-Gymnasium*

*Hauptschule : Gymnasium - Your teacher will explain the difference.

Bitte diese Beispiele ansehen

Look at these examples.

```
                    das Buch
Thomas bringt ein Buch mit.

               den   Kuli
Monika nimmt einen Kuli.

               die  Postkarte
Sie schreibt eine Postkarte.
```

Ü9   Bitte die Sätze ergänzen: einen – ein – eine
What should it be?

o Ich finde das Deutschheft nicht!

● Hier, ich habe _____ Heft.

o Klaus, findest du die Gitarre
nicht?

● Nein, ich nehme _____ Cassette.

o Macht ihr Hausaufgaben?

● Nein, wir schreiben _____ Karte.

o Ich habe den Kuli nicht!

● Na gut, ich nehme _____ Bleistift.

o Haben wir morgen Sport?
Nehmen wir den Fußball mit?

● Moment, ich habe _____ Stundenplan.

Ü10   *Now try this exercise.*

den – das – die – *what should it be?*

o Hast du meinen Atlas?

● Nein, hier nimm _____.

o Habt ihr eine Karte?

● Ja, nimm _____.

o Möchtest du meinen Stuhl?
(Would you like)

● Nein, ich nehme _____.

o Bringt ihr ein Radio mit?

● Nein, wir nehmen _____.

o Möchtest du eine Cola?

● Ja gut, ich nehme _____.

Schreibe mehr Fragen und Antworten

Write more questions and answers and practise with a friend.

4C

Bitte diese Beispiele ansehen

der Bleistift?   Der Bleistift?   Der ist hier.

Wo ist das Heft?   Das Heft? Das ist da.

die Karte?

Die Karte? Die ist hier rechts.

den Kuli? Monika?   Ja, sie hat den Kuli.

Wer hat das Buch? Du?   Nein, ich habe das Buch nicht.

die Tasche? Peter?   Ja, er hat die Tasche.

Ü11 Bitte ausfüllen

Fill in the missing words (= the definite articles)

Hier ist _____ Kuli. Wo hast du _____ Atlas? - Ich weiß nicht.

Das sind _____ Cassetten. Habt ihr _____ Gitarre? - Nein, leider nicht.

Wo ist _____ Ball? Wer hat _____ Stundenplan? - Ich nicht.

Ü12 Was nehme ich mit?

Peter gives an account in German of the things he has to take to school tomorrow Tuesday. What is missing in what he says?

Dienstag habe ich Mathematik, Sport, Deutsch

und Geographie.

Ich nehme _____ Mathebuch,

_____ Turnzeug und _____ Fußball,

_____ Deutschheft und _____ Atlas mit.

56

Ü13 **Eine Party**

Party-time! What are all these people doing?
Choose from the words in the list and use ein - eine - einen.

Hans nimmt _____

_____

Eva möchte _____

_____

Karin hat _____

_____

Klaus tanzt _____

_____

Peter hat _____

_____

Emine macht _____

_____

das Foto - die Limonade - der Luftballon - der Hit - der Hamburger - die Cassette

Ü14 **Bitte ausfüllen** *Can you complete this exercise with the correct form of:*

e i n / e / n   k e i n / e / n
                                 (= no / what you don't have)?

o Hast du _____ Karte?   ● Nein, ich habe _____ Karte.

o Ich nehme _____ Heft mit.   ● Ich nicht, ich habe _____ Heft.

o Bringt ihr _____ Gitarre mit? ● Nein, wir haben _____ Gitarre.

o Hast du _____ Kuli?   ● Nein, frag Klaus, ich habe _____ Kuli.

Dann nehme ich _____ Bleistift.

o Haben wir am Montag Sport?   ● Ja, aber Sport macht _____ Spaß!

Ü15 dein/deine/deinen

1. Hast du _____ Tasche? 2. Bitte schlage _____ Buch auf!

3. Wir schreiben _____ Stundenplan ab (abschreiben = copy).

4. Ich nehme _____ Karte. 5. Wo habe ich _____ Atlas?

Ü16 Minidialoge schreiben

This is a scramble of sentences. Try to put some order into what two schoolfriends have been saying.

Wo ist mein Kuli? Haben wir Freitag Sport?

Ich weiß nicht. Wo ist mein Stundenplan?

Oh, ich habe kein Das finde ich auch!

Nein, Freitag nicht. Englischheft.

Danke! Sport macht keinen Spaß!

Keine Ahnung. Nimm meinen Morgen haben wir Englisch.
Bleistift.

1. ● Wo ist mein Stundenplan?

   ○ Ich weiß nicht.

2. ● _____

   ○ _____

3. ● _____

   ○ _____

4. ● _____

   ○ _____

Ü17 Was tut Bettina hier?

Here's Bettina. What is she doing?

herausnehmen

1. Sie _____ ein Buch _____ .

aufschlagen

2. Sie _____ das Buch _____ .

mitnehmen

3. Sie _____ das Buch _____ .

Ü18 Imperativformen im Plural

Your German teacher asks you to do the following. What would he say to all of you in a more polite way?

1. das Deutschbuch herausnehmen

Beispiel: *Nehmt bitte das Deutschbuch heraus!* _____

2. den Satz mitschreiben

_____

3. die Hausaufgaben machen

_____

Ü 19 Imperativformen im Singular

What would a friend say to you? Choose from the following words.

Cassette   Fünfmarkstück   mitbringen   mitnehmen

Freund   herausnehmen

1. Bitte, *nimm deine Cassette heraus !*

2. _____

3. _____

Ü 20 Einen Stundenplan schreiben

Write your ideal timetable. Don't forget the days of the week.

					Samstag

Going to school in Germany

If you stay with a German family one of the most interesting things to do is to spend a day or two going to a German school (honestly!).

You would notice many differences compared with your school.

For example: lessons start early, at about 8.00 a.m.
In some parts of Germany school starts even earlier in the summer months.

Because school starts early, it also finishes early - usually by 1 p.m.
But it is a long hard morning. You might also have to go to school on Saturday mornings.

In the afternoon, there are often voluntary activities or clubs for such things as sport, drama, cooking, etc.

Did you know?

If the temperature in the classroom reaches 28°C, the school closes and everybody goes home! This is called "hitzefrei".

There are other interesting differences you would notice also. German pupils do not wear school uniform - although they often end up wearing the same sort of clothes as their friends anyway. What do you think about school uniform?

In some parts of Germany, there are now whole day schools, so-called "Ganztagsschulen". There are arguments for and against the traditional "half-day" schools. Can you think of points for and against?

4 Landeskunde

Every school has a school council (Schülermitverwaltung) known as the SMV. Each class elects pupil representatives (Klassensprecher) to sit on this council. The school council looks after the interests of the pupils. It even sends representatives to Staff Meetings, and also organises social events.

German pupils are always worried about their marks or grades. Individual pieces of work are marked on a scale from 1 (very good) to 6 (unsatisfactory) and the grades on the school report follow the same system. If you have 5's or 6's in main subjects you may have to stay down a year ("sitzenbleiben"). That means that all your friends go up to the next class while you remain where you were and are joined by a class of younger pupils. Your school grades are, of course, very important to you when you leave and apply for a job and/or a place at university.

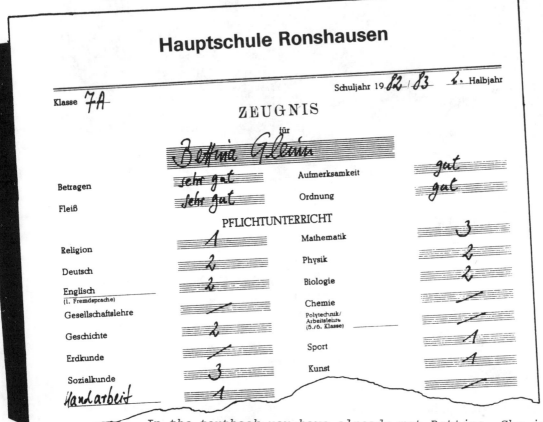

In the textbook you have already met Bettina. She is 13 years old. In Germany you start school at the age of 6.

Ü1 **Auf dem Campingplatz**

Bitte einen Dialog schreiben

Make a conversation to go with the picture.

Aus Holland. Woher kommst du?

Ja, gerne. Das macht Spaß.

Tag, Rita. Woher kommt ihr?

Guten Tag! Ich heiße Piet. Das hier ist Rita.

Aus Klagenfurt in Österreich.

Wir gehen schwimmen. Kommst du mit?

Hallo, ich heiße Wolfgang, und du?

_____

_____

_____

_____

_____

_____

Leute treffen *Meeting People - Complete these conversations.*

Kevin Morrison,   Sharon Field,   Resi Bauer,
17, Derby   16, Nottingham   16, Linz

Paul Riz,   Jeanne Sue,   Renate Merten,
16, Montpellier   15   14, Koblenz

_____ _____ Hein Hansen,
                                   Buxtehude

_____ _____

Ü 2 **Bitte die Dialoge
① bis ③ schreiben**

① Begrüßen, Vorstellen
   ↓
   Woher?

● Guten Tag, ich heiße
  Kevin Morrison.
  Das ist .....

o Mein Name ist Resi
  Bauer .....

② Begrüßen, Vorstellen
   ↓
   Woher? → Wo?

● Hallo, ich heiße .....

o .....

③ Begrüßen, Vorstellen
   ↓
   Woher? → Wo?
   ↓   ↙
   Alter?
   ↓
   ?

● Guten Tag, ...

o .....

Ü3 Interviews

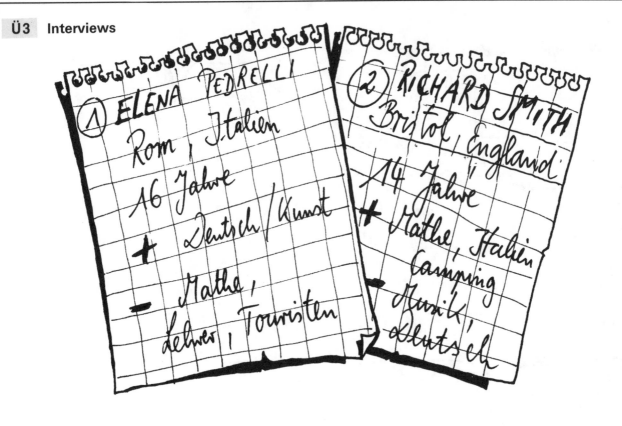

① ELENA PEDRELLI
Rom, Italien
16 Jahre
+ Deutsch / Kunst
– Mathe,
Lehrer, Touristen

② RICHARD SMITH
Bristol, England
14 Jahre
+ Mathe, Italien
Camping
Musik,
Deutsch

You have interviewed these people and made notes about them. Can you now write a full account of each one and say who he/she is and what he/she dislikes?

Sie heißt Elena Pedrelli. Sie ...

Revision

1 **Was sagen sie?** *What are they saying?*

Ich.....
.....Irland.
Woher.....
?

Ich.....
München.

.....du?

Mein
.....Carla.

Hallo,.....
Nick.
.....Amsterdam.

Ich.....
.....Montreal.

Ich.....
und das.....
Wie.....
?

Ich.....
und.....
.....Amerika.

2 **Fragen schreiben**

Write out 5 questions to Rocky.

(heißen) W_____?

(sein) W_____?

(kommen) W_____?

(wohnen) W_____?

W_____?

3 Was kostet ein/eine .....? Ein/eine ..... kostet ....
Was kosten zwei ....? Zwei ..... kosten ....

Write out how much these things would cost.

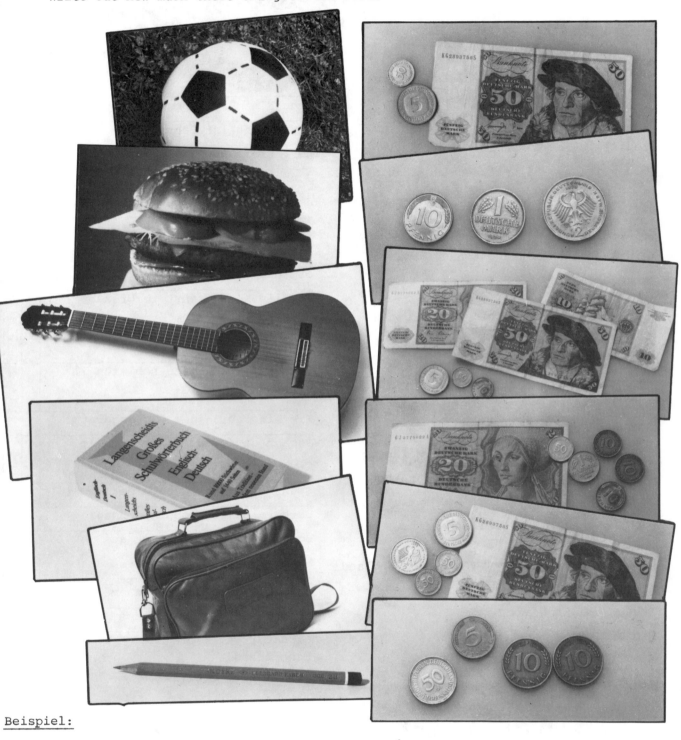

Beispiel:

Ein Fußball kostet fünfundfünfzig Mark fünfzig.

Ein......

4 Familie Klein macht Urlaub

Richtig oder falsch?
True or false?

Das ist Familie Klein.
Herr Klein ist Ingenieur.
Frau Klein ist Lehrerin.
Jochen ist 14. Seine Schwester Claudia 12.

Sie wohnen in Pullach bei München.
Familie Klein hat einen Caravan.
Im Urlaub fahren sie oft nach England
ans Meer.

Diesmal sind sie auf einem Campingplatz
in Kent. Jochen und Claudia haben ein
Zelt. Herr und Frau Klein schlafen im
Caravan.

Auf dem Campingplatz gibt es viele junge
Leute: Da ist Franz Bauer aus Salzburg
in Österreich. Er ist 13. Barbara Hohler
kommt aus Basel. Bernard Goldstein wohnt
in Colmar. Das ist in Frankreich.

Die meisten jungen Leute sind aus England:
Gary, 15, ist aus Dagenham.
Tracey, 14, ist aus Leeds.
Richard, 14, wohnt in Bristol.

	r	f
Frau Klein ist Ingenieurin.		
Herr Klein ist Lehrer.		
Herr Klein ist Ingenieur.		
Jochen hat keine Schwester.		
Jochen ist 14 Jahre alt.		
Claudia ist dreizehn Jahre alt.		
Familie Klein fährt im Urlaub oft nach Österreich.		
Familie Klein fährt im Urlaub oft ans Meer.		
Sie fahren nach München.		
Herr und Frau Klein schlafen im Zelt.		
Sie sind auf einem Campingplatz.		
Jochen und Claudia schlafen im Caravan.		
Franz Bauer ist aus Colmar.		
Barbara Hohler wohnt in Basel.		
Bernard Goldstein kommt aus Hamburg.		
Gary, 15, ist aus Dagenham.		
Tracey, 14, ist aus Leeds.		
Richard, 14, kommt aus Schottland.		

5 Richtig oder falsch?

GELDWECHSLER WECHSELT

0.50 DM in 5 x 10 Pf.
1.- DM in 5 x 10 Pf. + 1 x 50 Pf.
2.- DM in 5 x 10 Pf. + 1 x 50 Pf. + 1 x 1,- DM

Der Geldwechsler wechselt .....

	r	f
..... 0,50 DM in 10 x 5 Pf.		
..... 1,-- DM in 5 x 10 Pf. + 1 x 50 Pf.		
..... 2,-- DM in 5 x 10 Pf. + 2 x 50 Pf. + 1 x 1,-- DM		

6 **Bitte die Verben einsetzen** *Fill in the correct form of the verbs.*

a) kommen

Woher _____ du?

Woher _____ ihr?

Woher _____ sie?

Ich _____ aus Frankfurt.

Er _____ aus Verona.

Sie _____ aus Hamburg.

b) heißen

Wie _____ du?

Ich _____ .

Er _____ Klaus.

Sie _____ Anna.

Wie _____ Sie?

Wie _____ er?

c) wohnen

Ich _____ in Kassel.

Er _____ in Rom.

Sie _____ in Paris.

W _____ du?

W _____ er?

W _____ ihr?

W _____ sie?

d) mitbringen

Er _____ einen Bleistift

_____ .

Ich _____ eine Cola _____ .

Tina _____ ein Buch _____ .

Marc und Bettina _____

deine Tasche _____ .

Ich _____ Hamburger _____ .

7 **Bitte ergänzen** *Verb endings please!*

1. Wie heiß____ Sie? Woher komm____ Sie? Wo wohn____ Sie? – 2. Ich heiß____

Olav Nordli. Ich komm____ aus Norwegen. Ich wohn____ in Bergen. – 3. Ich

heiß____ Akira. Das ____ Frau Yashima. Wir komm____ aus Japan. Wir wohn____

in Osaka. – 4. Ich heiß____ Resi Bauer. Ich komm____ aus Österreich. Ich

wohn____ in Linz. – 5. Das ____ Herr Mbawi Kano. Er komm____ aus Nigeria.

Er wohn____ in Lagos. – 6. Das ____ Fräulein Jeanne Sue. Sie komm____ aus

Frankreich. Sie wohn____ in Montpellier. – 7. Wir heiß____ Bente Juul und

Hanne Jensen. Wir komm____ aus Dänemark. Wir wohn____ in Odense.

1-4C Wiederholung

8 Verben – Artikel – Pronomen

a) mein – dein – unser

ich: Das ist _____ Ball, _____ Cassette, _____ Kuli,

_____ Tasche, _____ Gitarre.

du: Ist das _____ Atlas, _____ Fünfmarkstück,

_____ Stuhl, _____ Buch?

wir: Das ist _____ Tisch, _____ Landkarte, _____

Klasse, _____ Lehrer.

b) mitbringen/ein

Er _____ _____ Bleistift _____.

Ich _____ _____ Cola _____.

Beate _____ _____ Buch _____.

Marc und Bettina _____ _____ Tasche _____.

Ich _____ _____ Hamburger _____.

c) haben – mitbringen/ein/mein – dein – unser

_____ du e_____ Stuhl? Bitte, _____ d_____ Stuhl _____.

Marc und Bettina _____ Cassetten _____. Sie _____ auch

e_____ Gitarre _____. Wir _____ u_____ Freund Klaus _____.

Er _____ m_____ Deutschbuch _____. Ich _____ m_____

Schwester und m_____ Bruder _____.

70

d) sein – haben/der, den, das, die

Hier _____ _____ Stundenplan. Wo _____ du _____ Karte?

Wo _____ ihr _____ Englischbuch? Und wo _____ _____ Turnschuhe?

Ich finde _____ Atlas nicht. _____ Heft _____ hier. Ich _____

_____ Kuli und _____ Bleistift.

9 Sätze schreiben

Write correct sentences using den/das/die.

Florian - Paß - herausnehmen _____ *Florian* _____

Maria und Eva - Cassetten - mitbringen _____

Astrid - Mathebuch - aufschlagen _____

10 Wörter und Zahlen kombinieren

Can you match the numbers with some of the words?
Check plural endings in chapter 3.

7	2	4	9	18	17	37	21
24	6	11	15	29	16	22	

Freund   Nummer   Schwester   Lehrer   Lineal   Tisch

Tourist   Mädchen   Stuhl   Bleistift   Gitarre

Radiergummi   Tasche   Cassette   Ball

11 Vier Länder

From which countries do these people come? The German names of the countries are hidden in their names. Can you find them by rearranging the letters?

ERICH KNARF   PAUL TROG   ERICH RÖSTE   JNA STRAULE

12 **Rechtschreibung** *Spelling exercise. Write out the words in full.*

Er hei ① Wolfram und ist aus
Österr ② ch. Er fin ③ t Französi ④,
Ma ⑤ ematik, Sport und Reli ⑥ on gut.
Engl ⑦ h, Kun ⑧ und P ⑨ sik fin ⑩
er lang ⑪ lig. Er hat oft Haus ⑫ fgaben
auf. Er sp ⑬ lt gern Fu ⑭ ball. Wolf-
ram hat eine Gitarre. Er is ⑮ fünfzehn
J ⑯ re alt. Er hat eine Sch ⑰ ster.

1._____ 2._____

3._____ 4._____

5._____ 6._____

7._____ 8._____

9._____ 10._____

11._____ 12._____

13._____ 14._____

15._____ 16._____

17._____

Bettina geht in die ① ule. Sie ni ② t
die Ta ③ e mit. Sie hat einen Blei ④ ift,
einen Kul ⑤, drei He ⑥ te, das De ⑦ ch-
buch, das Ma ⑧ ebuch und den A ⑨ las.
Sie geht in die Klasse 7a. Sie findet
Deutsch Sp ⑩ e, aber Sport la ⑪ -
weilig. Sie findet den Lehrer inter-
e ⑫ ant. Montag nimmt sie ihr Turn-
z ⑬ g mit.

1._____ 2._____

3._____ 4._____

5._____ 6._____

7._____ 8._____

9._____ 10._____

11._____ 12._____

13._____

13 **Schreibe einige Sätze über einen Freund/eine Freundin**

*Try to write a few sentences about a friend. Your classmates should then find
out who he or she is.
The following hints will help you: age - hometown - subjects he/she likes
or dislikes - hobbies.*

_____

_____

_____

_____

Ü1 **Bitte ausfüllen**

Draw a picture of yourself.

Now fill in your details:

Name: _____

Alter: _____

Größe: _____

Haare: _____

Augen: _____

Geschwister: _____

Hobbys: _____

Lieblingsfächer: _____

Ü2 **Sich selbst vorstellen**

*Using the information from exercise 1 write a short description of yourself –
for example:*

Ich heiße John Smith.

Ich bin 13 (Jahre alt). etc.

| *Useful phrases:* Meine Haare sind ... |
| Ich habe ... |
| Meine Hobbys sind ... |

Ich _____

_____

_____

_____

_____

_____

Ü3 Interviewe deinen Partner

Now interview your partner. Ask him/her the following questions:

Wie heißt du? Wie alt bist du? Wie groß bist du? Wie sind deine Haare?

Wie sind deine Augen? Hast du Geschwister? Was sind deine Hobbys?

Was sind deine Lieblingsfächer?

Name: _____

Alter: _____

Größe: _____

Haare: _____

Augen: _____

Geschwister: _____

Hobbys: _____

Lieblingsfächer: _____

Ü4 Bitte berichten

Now please report:

> *Useful phrases:*
>
> Mein Freund/Meine Freundin heißt ...
>
> Er/sie ist ...
>
> Seine/Ihre Haare sind ...
>
> Er/Sie hat ...

_____

_____

_____

_____

_____

_____

Ü5 **Briefe schreiben** *Write letters to Kirsten and Klaus telling them all about Dieter and Bettina.*

① Dieter Goedecke

Alter: 15 Jahre
Größe: 1,72 m
Haare: braun
Augen: blau
Geschwister: 1 Bruder,
              1 Schwester
Hobbys: Musik hören
Lieblingsfächer: Sport,
                  Englisch

Liebe Kirsten!
das ist mein Freund Dieter. Er ist .....
Seine .....

② Bettina Tscholl

Alter: 14 Jahre
Größe: 1,64 m
Haare: dunkelbraun
Augen: blaugrün
Geschwister: 1 Bruder,
              1 Schwester
Hobbys: Lesen
Lieblingsfächer: Deutsch,
                  Englisch

Lieber Klaus,
das ist ein Bild von Bettina.
Sie ist meine Freundin. Ich finde .....

Sie ist .....
Bettina mag .....

Dein Freund
Peter

6A

Ü6 **Wie heißen diese Sportarten?** *Can you remember the German words for these sports?*

Ü7 Hobbies – *Find out what they are and write the German expressions underneath each picture.*

Schwimmen   Tanzen   Fußball spielen   Radfahren   Reiten

Lesen   Briefmarken sammeln   Skilaufen   Singen

Handball spielen   ins Kino gehen   Badminton spielen

Und was sind deine Hobbys? *What are your favourite hobbies?*

Ü8

Schüler schreiben an »treff«

Here are some letters from young Germans who are looking for pen-friends. Read them carefully and write the main points of information into the grid below.

Brieffreundschaften

Hallo "treff"! Ich bin 13 Jahre alt und suche eine(n) Brief-freund(in) im Alter zwischen 13 und 15 Jahren. Möglichst aus Berlin. Meine Hobbys sind: Schwimmen, Tanzen und Brief-marken.
Hans Bergmann, Nürnberg

Hallo, Mädchen! Ich suche eine Brieffreundin (12 oder 13 Jahre alt). Ich habe die Hobbys: Lesen, Schwimmen, Briefe schreiben. Ich bin 13 Jahre alt. Schreibt mit Foto an:
Jürgen Oehler, Kiel

Ich (13 Jahre) suche eine Brieffreundin, die auch etwa 13 ist. Ich inter-essiere mich für Hunde, Lesen, Popmusik, Klavier-spielen und Englisch. Ich beantworte alle Briefe. Wenn möglich: schreibt in Englisch!
Gisela Tönning, Konstanz

Suche Brieffreund(in) im Alter von 11 bis 15 Jahren. Ich bin 14 Jahre. Meine Hobbys: Reiten, Tiere, Radfahren, Musik und vieles mehr.
... Nehmt doch einen Stift und schreibt mir. Ich würde mich sehr freuen.
Karin Buch, Köln

*

Ich (12) suche eine Brief-freundin, die in der Schweiz oder in Österreich wohnt. Meine Hobbys: Lesen, Gitarre, Flöte, Volleyball, Briefmar-ken, Tischtennis. Außerdem mag ich Tiere gern. Bitte Foto mitschicken.
Monika Haug, München-Solln

*

Hallihallo! Suche Brief-freundin im Alter von 12 bis 14, bin 13 Jahre alt. Hobbys: Tennis, Lesen, Tiere, Popmusik. Bitte Foto beilegen.
Heidi Wagner, Waldenburg

("treff" is a pupils' magazine)

Notes:

Name	Age	Hometown	Age of penfriend	Hobbies
1.				
2.				
3.				
4.				
5.				
6.				

Ü9 **Eine Anzeige schreiben**

*Imagine you are looking for a German pen-friend in a German magazine.
Write an advertisement.*

Suche

Ich bin

Meine Hobbys

Briefe an:

Ü10 **Farben**

*Write the German names of the colours in the flags and then colour
in your paintbox.*

grün - rot - blau - gelb - braun - rosa - orange - lila - schwarz - weiß -
grau - türkis

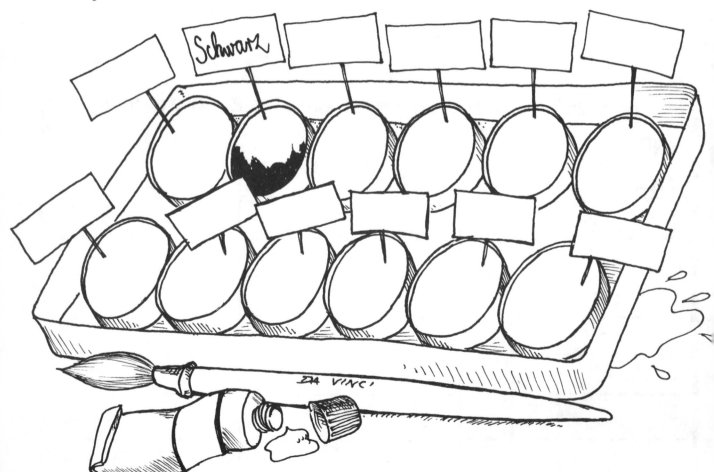

Schwarz

Ü11 Meinungen zum Schulsport

a) *What changes would these German pupils like to see in their PE lessons?*
Can you match 2-5 and a, b, d, e as the example shows?

Ich finde nicht gut, daß wir so selten
Trampolin springen.   Petra

Am Ende der Stunde sollten wir immer
ein Spiel machen.

Am besten finde ich Weitspringen und
Weitwerfen. Ich würde es auch besser
finden, wenn wir im Sommer Federball
oder Fußball spielen würden.
                              Heiko

Ich finde Sportunterricht in der Schule
nicht gut, denn wenn man nichts richtig
macht, lachen die anderen. Mir gefällt
aber, daß wir zehn Minuten machen dürfen,
was wir wollen.   Susanne

Gut finde ich, daß ich in den Umkleide-
raum gehen kann, wenn ich keine Lust
mehr habe. Schlecht finde ich, daß es
überhaupt Sportunterricht gibt.
                              Armin

... was mir nicht gefällt, ist, daß wir
duschen müssen (müssen!). Mir gefällt
es aber, daß wir zwei Stunden Sport
haben!   Christian

Manchmal ist der Unterricht langweilig,
wenn man jede Stunde dasselbe macht.
Man müßte Musik zum Sportunterricht
machen (aber keine Disco-Songs). Ich
meine, dann macht der Sportunterricht
mehr Spaß.   Birgit

Es ist schade, daß wir nur zwei Stunden
Sport haben und kaum Spiele machen.
                              Annegret

1. Petra

2. Christian

3. Annegret

4. Heiko

5. Birgit

a) mehr Spiele

b) Sport mit Musik

c) mehr Trampolin springen

d) am Ende nicht duschen müssen

e) im Sommer Fußball und Badminton

1				
C				

*duschen = take a shower

b) *Can you spot these opinions in the text?*
Who said what? Put the right letter against each of the names.

a) If we do the same thing every lesson it sometimes becomes boring.

b) A pity we only have two PE lessons a week.

c) We ought to finish each lesson with a game.

d) A good thing I can go to the changing room if I don't feel like it any more.

e) I like the two PE lessons.

f) If you don't do everything the right way the others laugh at you.

Birgit	☐	Heiko	☐
Christian	☐	Annegret	☐
Susanne	☐	Armin	☐

Keep fit!

In order to fill in 1 square on the spiral you would need to do 60 minutes of walking or gardening but only 5 minutes of intensive fitness training.

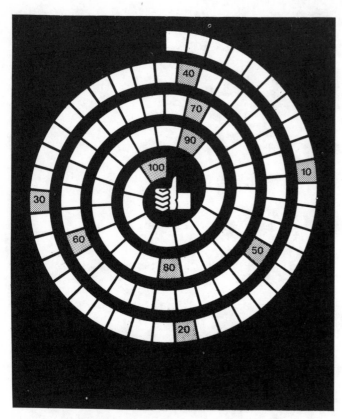

5 Min.	L	Dauerlauf
	KT	Konditionstraining
10 Min.	S	Schwimmen
15 Min.	R	Radfahren
	G	Gymnastik
	T	Turnen
	SL	Skilaufen
	F	Fußball
	VB	Volleyball
	FB	Badminton
	TE	Tennis
	E	Eislaufen
	HB	Handball
	RK	Rudern Kanu
30 Min.	TT	Tischtennis
	B	Bergsteigen
	RE	Reiten
	TA	Tanzen
60 Min.	W	Wandern
	GA	Gartenarbeit

After 5 minutes of Dauerlauf (L) you can fill in 1 square.
Now fill in the names of the other sports in the list.

Ü12 **Bitte ausfüllen**

 5 Minuten L =   30 Minuten TT =

10 Minuten S =   TA =

15 Minuten R =   60 Minuten W =

15 Minuten HB =

Wie findest du "TT"?

Was machst du am liebsten?

Ü13 **Bitte ergänzen: spielen/finden/sich interessieren/haben**

1. o Spielst du gern Handball? • Nein, ich _____ Handballspielen blöd.

2. o Ich _____ gern Fußball. • Ich mag Judo lieber.

3. o Und Tina? • Sie _____ gern Tennis.

4. o _____ du eine Schwester? • Nein, ich _____ einen Bruder.

5. o Unser Lehrer _____ _____ für Bogenschießen. • Ich _____ Bogenschießen langweilig.

6. o Wir _____ _____ für Leichtathletik. • Wir _____ Tischtennis besser.

Ü14 **Hobbys**

sich für etwas interessieren

Petra und Marc interessieren _____ _____ Musik.

Dieter _____ _____ sehr _____ Sport, aber nicht _____ Mathematik.

_____ du _____ _____ Fußball?

Ich _____ _____ gar nicht _____ Sport!

Ü15 **Bitte ergänzen: gern? – gut?**

a) Ich habe meinen Hund _____, aber Katzen mag ich überhaupt nicht.

   Hunde finde ich wirklich _____!

b) Mein Bruder findet den Mathelehrer _____. Ich habe den Sportlehrer _____. Er ist wirklich _____.

c) Klaus hat Martina _____. Das finde ich nicht _____. Sie ist doch meine Freundin.

Ü16 **Fragen schreiben**

Fragen:	Antworten:
_____?	Ich heiße Ertürk Hassan.
_____?	Ich bin 15.
_____?	Ich wohne in Remscheid.
_____?	Ich spiele gern Fußball.
_____?	Ich mag das Fach Sport.

Ü17 **Setze die richtigen Formen ein**

Fill in the right words.

gern ♡	gut ✚
lieber ♡♡	besser ✚✚
am liebsten! ♡♡♡	am besten! ✚✚✚

1. Wen magst du ♡ ?
   Ich habe Tracey ♡ .
   Tracey hat Kevin ♡♡ !

2. Bayern München spielt ✚ .
   Juventus spielt ✚✚ -
   Ja, aber Liverpool spielt ✚✚✚ !

3. Ich spiele ♡♡ Handball - Judo mag ich ♡♡♡ .
   Ich finde, Hockey ist ✚✚✚ .
   Was magst du ♡♡♡ ?

Now write them out in full:

1. Wen magst du gern?

   _____

   _____!

2. Bayern München _____ .

   _____ !

3. Ich spiele _____ - _____ .

   _____ .

   _____ ?

Ü18 **Fragen schreiben**

It's Conny's first day at school. Which questions might she ask another pupil?

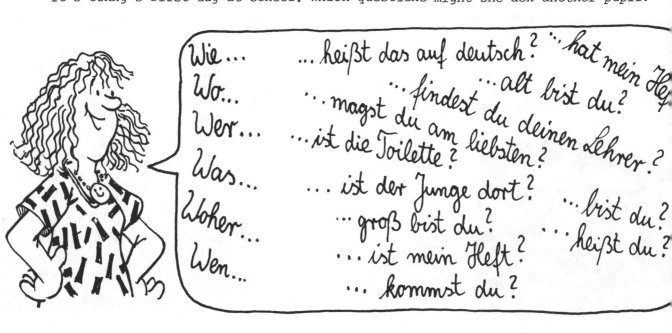

Wie...   ...heißt das auf deutsch?   ...hat mein He[ft]
Wo...   ...findest du deinen Lehrer?   ...alt bist du?
Wer...   ...magst du am liebsten?
                ...ist die Toilette?
Was...   ... ist der Junge dort?   ...bist du?
Woher...   ...groß bist du?   ...heißt du?
Wen...   ...ist mein Heft?
                ... kommst du?

Sport

Most people are involved with sports at school or in clubs. Many more are spectators or simply watch on television. There is wide coverage of sports on television especially on Saturday and Sunday. Highlights of the football matches in the "Bundesliga" (Federal League, 1st Division) are shown soon after the matches finish. A lot of time is given to other sports too.

Taking part

Many young people belong to clubs - remember there is normally no school in the afternoons. Some sports such as skiing are very popular but most people who go on skiing holidays do not belong to clubs. However, if we judge the popularity of different sports in Germany by the numbers of people who belong to clubs we get some interesting and surprising results.

For example, see if you can guess the right order of popularity of these sports in Germany:

(a) Shooting   (b) Soccer   (c) Horse Riding   (d) Cycling   (e) Basketball
(f) Gymnastics (g) Swimming (h) Judo   (i) Athletics (j) Handball

1. _____

2. _____

3. _____

4. _____

5. _____

6. _____

7. _____

8. _____

9. _____

10. _____

Here are the answers:

1 b
2 f
3 a
4 i
5 g
6 j
7 c
8 h
9 d
10 e

Profis

I. Bundesliga

Arminia Bielefeld – Bayer Leverkusen				0:2	(0:0)
Eintracht Frankfurt – Karlsruher SC				2:0	(2:0)
VfL Bochum – Fortuna Düsseldorf				3:1	(0:0)
Bayern München – Werder Bremen				1:1	(1:0)
Hamburger SV – 1. FC Nürnberg				3:0	(3:0)
Mönchengladbach – FC Schalke 04				0:0	
VfB Stuttgart – Borussia Dortmund				2:1	(1:0)
Hertha BSC – 1. FC Kaiserslautern				0:0	
1. FC Köln – Eintr. Braunschweig				3:1	(1:0)

1	Hamburger SV	18	10	8	0	45:17	28:8
2	Bayern München	18	10	5	3	37:13	25:11
3	VfB Stuttgart	18	10	4	4	41:23	24:12
4	1. FC Köln	18	10	4	4	35:20	24:12
5	Werder Bremen	18	10	4	4	32:20	24:12
6	Borussia Dortmund	18	10	3	5	41:26	23:13
7	1. FC Kaiserslautern	18	6	9	3	25:21	21:15
8	Arminia Bielefeld	18	7	4	7	30:38	18:18
9	Eintr. Braunschweig	18	5	6	7	18:29	16:20
10	1. FC Nürnberg	18	6	4	8	22:34	16:20
11	VfL Bochum	18	5	5	8	21:26	15:21
12	Eintracht Frankfurt	18	6	2	10	26:26	14:22
13	Mönchengladbach	18	6	2	10	31:35	14:22
14	Fortuna Düsseldorf	18	4	6	8	30:45	14:22
15	Hertha BSC	18	3	7	8	19:29	13:23
16	Karlsruher SC	18	4	4	10	24:43	12:24
17	Bayer Leverkusen	18	4	4	10	16:35	12:24
18	FC Schalke 04	18	3	5	10	23:36	11:25

Die nächsten Spiele (Samstag, 15.30 Uhr): Kaiserslautern – Köln, Schalke – Stuttgart, Nürnberg – Mönchengladbach, Bremen – Hamburg, Düsseldorf – FC Bayern, Karlsruhe – Bochum, Leverkusen – Frankfurt, Braunschweig – Bielefeld, Dortmund – Hertha BSC.

International Sport

West Germany (the Federal Republic) always has a very strong national football team, both at youth and at full international level. Their men and women athletes often win medals and they are also good at winter sports and horse-riding for example.

East Germany (the Democratic Republic) is always very successful in winning medals at the Olympic Games. East German athletes, swimmers and skaters are especially good. You must have seen them on television.

Austria and Switzerland too have good football teams and some well known sportsmen and women. But their most popular athletes usually are skiers and ski-jumpers.

Kanufahren

Segeln

Eisschnellaufen

Things to find out

a) What is Handball?
b) In which year did Germany win the World Cup (Football)?
c) Which areas of Germany are popular for winter sports?
d) Name some famous German racing cars.
e) In which winter sports events have the Austrians and the Swiss been successful in recent years?
f) When have the Olympic Games been held in Germany?

Ü1 Wann hast du Zeit?

You are trying to arrange with your friend when to go swimming. Look at the opening times and then complete the conversation.

Useful phrases:

+ Ja, das geht. Gut, einverstanden. O.K. Prima, das geht.

- Nein, das geht nicht. Schade. Da geht's nicht.

Gehen wir ins Schwimmbad?   +   Ja, wann denn? _____

           Am Sonntag?   -   _____

Sagen wir am Samstag um 16 Uhr.

Geht das?   -   _____

Am Freitag um 16 Uhr?   +   _____

O.K., dann gehen wir am Freitag.   _____

Now add some more questions and answers of your own.

_____   _____

_____   _____

_____   _____

_____   _____

_____   _____

Ü2 **Dialoge üben und schreiben**

Here are two conversations starting with the same question. Practise them with a partner and see how they turn out. Then do two conversations of your own and practise them too.

a) o Wir spielen Tischtennis. Kommst du mit?

● Prima! Wann denn?   ● Wann gehen wir?

o Am Dienstag um 14 Uhr.   o Um 2.

● Ja, das geht.   ● Wie lange spielen wir?

o Tschüs bis Dienstag.   o Zwei Stunden von 14 bis 16 Uhr.

                                       ● Nein, das geht nicht.

                                       o Warum nicht?

                                       ● Ich spiele um 15 Uhr Basketball.

                                       o Kannst du am Samstag?

                                       ● Ja, das geht. Wann denn?

                                       o Um 2.

                                       ● Gut, einverstanden. Tschüs.

                                       o Tschüs bis Samstag.

b) o Wir gehen schwimmen. Kommst du mit?

● (+?) _____   ● (?) _____

o (Fr. 13 Uhr) _____   o (4) _____

● (+) _____   ● (?) _____

o _____   o (1/2 16 - 16.30) _____

                                       ● (-) _____

                                       o (?) _____

                                       ● (16.30 Fußball) _____

                                       o (Mi.?) _____

                                       ● (+?) _____

                                       o (8) _____

                                       ● (+) _____

                                       o _____

c) *Now write a conversation on your own. The textbook will give you some ideas if you need them. The conversation starts:*

o Kommst du am Samstag tanzen?

● _____

o _____

● _____

o _____

● _____

Ü3 Ein Wochenende: Bitte aufschreiben

Fill in your diary.

7B

Ü4 Uhrzeiten

Wie spät ist es bitte?

_____

Wann beginnt die Schule?

_____

Wann kommst du?

_____

Wann spielt ihr Tennis?

_____

Ü5

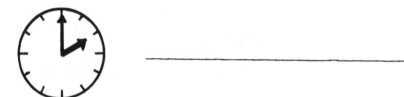

...Mitternacht!

„Ihr Zug-Begleiter" // "Your guide in the train"
Provides information about the schedule of this train

Ankunft Arrival		Abfahrt Departure
	München Hbf	16.43
18.57	Stuttgart Hbf	19.03
20.12	Heidelberg Hbf	20.14
22.57	Köln Hbf	23.01
0.18	Dortmund Hbf	

Von München um sechzehn Uhr dreiundvierzig
= vier Uhr dreiundvierzig

In Stuttgart um _____

= _____

In Heidelberg um _____

= _____

In Köln   um _____

= _____

In Dortmund um _____

= _____

Ü6 Uhrzeiten – Wie sagt man auf deutsch?

1.30 p.m. = Ein Uhr dreißig   = halb zwei

(Dreizehn Uhr dreißig)

2.45 p.m. = _____   = _____

(_____)

6.25 p.m. = _____   = _____

(_____)

8.40 p.m. = _____   = _____

(_____) _____

Ü7

a) *Read the text. Can you spot the answers to the questions on the right?*

Jörg Trachte, 15
Am liebsten immer Tischtennis

Mein Lieblingssport ist Tischtennis. Seit zwei Jahren spiele ich in einem Tischtennis-Verein. Ich habe mit 11 Jahren angefangen zu spielen. Jetzt bin ich schon zwei Jahre in der Jugendmannschaft. Training habe ich jeden Montag und Donnerstag.

Radfahren, Volleyballspielen und Musik hören finde ich auch gut. Aber am liebsten würde ich in meiner Freizeit nur Tischtennis spielen. Das kann ich aber leider nicht, weil wir zu Hause keinen Platz für eine Tischtennisplatte haben. Wir wohnen in einem Reihenhaus. Mein Vater ist Industriekaufmann, und meine Mutter ist Laborantin. Mein Bruder ist 13 Jahre und geht in ein Gymnasium.

In die Schule gehe ich nicht so gerne. Meine Lieblingsfächer sind Sport und Englisch. Mein Schulweg ist nicht weit. Ich fahre nur eine Haltestelle weiter mit der U-Bahn. Mit der U-Bahn fahre ich auch in die Stadt.

Steckbrief

(Personal description)

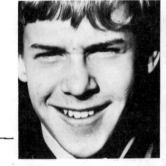

Alter? _____

Lieblingssport? _____

Wie viele Jahre? _____

Training: Wie oft? _____

     Wann? _____

     Wo? _____

Lieblingsfächer? _____

Schulweg? _____

Wohnung? _____

Bruder / Schwester? _____

b) *Now write a few sentences about Jörg. Use the key words above.*

c) *Try to give a similar description about yourself.*

Dein Schulweg: mit dem Bus? mit dem Rad? Ich gehe zu Fuß!

Jutta Mattheus (15)
Mein Freund und ich

Mein Freund heißt Michael, er ist 17 Jahre alt. Ich kenne ihn schon seit Jahren.

Wenn die Clique bei mir zu Hause ist, hören wir auch viel Musik. Um 19 Uhr müssen sie aber spätestens aus dem Haus sein, weil dann meine Eltern kommen.

Abends besuche ich gern meinen Freund. Samstags muß ich um halb zwölf spätestens zu Hause sein. Sonst aber schon um Viertel nach neun.

Mein Bruder ist 20 Jahre alt. Wir unternehmen viel, fahren mit seinem Motorrad weg. Am Wochenende fahren wir ins Grüne oder in die Diskothek.

Wochentags kann ich mit meinem Bruder leider nichts unternehmen.
Dreimal in der Woche habe ich Training.
In meiner restlichen Freizeit trinke ich mit meiner Clique Tee. Fast täglich kommen sie zu mir nach Hause.
Zweimal in der Woche gehe ich zu meinen Eltern ins Geschäft putzen.
Im Monat verdiene ich etwa 200 Mark. Der Job gefällt mir gut. Von dem Geld kaufe ich mir Klamotten, Jeans oder Pullover.

Ü8 **Bitte lesen und einsetzen**

Read this text. Then try to fill in the gaps.
You will find the missing words and information
in the text on the left.

Ihr _____ heißt Michael. Er ist ____ Jahre alt.

Sie _____ ihn _____ Jahren. Jutta _____

viel Musik mit der Clique. Ihre _____

kommen um _____ nach Hause. Abends besucht

sie gern ihren _____. Samstags muß sie um

_____ Uhr zu Hause sein. Sonst muß sie schon um

_____ zu Hause sein.

Ihr _____ ist 20 Jahre alt. Am Wochenende

_____

_____

_____ in der Woche hat Jutta Training. Oft

_____ sie mit ihrer _____ Tee. Sie ver-

dient im Monat etwa _____ und kauft sich

oft _____

Ü9 Wo man sich trifft

This is a list of places in a German town where young people can meet.

Jugendtreff
Piccolo-Club, Dachauer Str. 23 (Nähe Hbf.), Tel. 59 49 84
Mo–Fr 14.30–22.00 Uhr u. jeden 1. u. 3. Sonntag im Monat
von 15–19 Uhr
Sonntagstreff St. Paul, St.-Paul-Platz 10, Tel. 55 48 95,
So 15.00–18.30 Uhr
Internationaler Club – IN VIA, Klarastr. 10, Tel. 19 42 46,
Di 19–23 Uhr

Club Treffpunkt für junge Leute,
Marie-Luise-Schattenmann-Haus, Friedrich-Loy-Str. 16,
Tel. 3 00 85 84, Do ab 19.30 Uhr
Freizeitheim Alter Botanischer Garten,
Luisenstr. 11, Eingang Karlstr. (Nähe Hbf.), Tel. 55 51 49,
Di–Sa 13.30–21.00 Uhr

1. *Find out where you could go on a Thursday night.*

_____

_____

2. *How many times a week and on what days could you visit the "Freizeitheim"?*

_____

3. *Which club is open every Sunday?*

_____

Ü10 Viele Vorschläge für die Ferien

Can you write down in English what suggestions for holiday activities are made by these pictures? Make a list.

Museumsbesuche

Ein Picknick machen

Ein Modell bauen

Segelkurse

Ein Musikinstrument lernen

Ferien auf dem Bauernhof

Now add the <u>German</u> *expressions to your list.*

Ü11 Schreibe die Fragen: Wie spät ...? Wie lange ...? Wann ...? Wie oft ...?

Fragen:

1. <u>Wie oft spielst du Fußball?</u>
   (Fußball spielen)

2. _____?
   (Uhr?)

3. _____?
   (Mathe haben)

4. _____?
   (kommen)

5. _____?
   (Schule haben)

6. _____?
   (schwimmen gehen)

7. _____?
   (Party dauern)

Antworten:

- Zweimal in der Woche.

- Es ist kurz nach zehn.

- Viermal in der Woche.

- Ich komme um halb acht.

- Von acht bis eins.

- Um ein Uhr.

- Ich weiß nicht. Oft von acht bis 12 Uhr.

Ü12 Bitte einsetzen: mich – dich

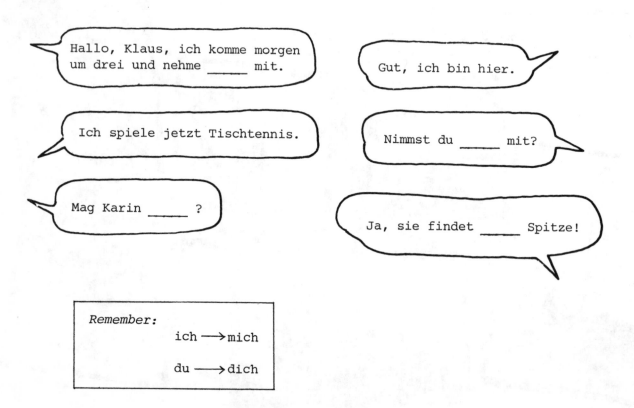

Hallo, Klaus, ich komme morgen um drei und nehme _____ mit.

Gut, ich bin hier.

Ich spiele jetzt Tischtennis.

Nimmst du _____ mit?

Mag Karin _____ ?

Ja, sie findet _____ Spitze!

Remember:

ich ⟶ mich

du ⟶ dich

Ü13 Bitte einsetzen: ihn – sie – es

Nehmt bitte das Deutschheft heraus
und schlagt _____ auf!

!.....

Hat Jörg einen Fußball?

Ja, er bringt _____ oft mit.

Ich finde die Gitarre Klasse!

Kaufe _____ doch!

Wie findest du Juttas Eltern?

Ich mag _____ sehr gern.

Was sagt er?

Ich verstehe _____ nicht.

Wie lange kennst du deine
Freundin Petra?

Ich kenne _____ seit Jahren.

Hast du das Training gern?

Ja, ich habe _____ sehr gern.

Remember: er ⟶ ihn
sie ⟶ sie
es ⟶ es

Ü14 Supermann und Lois Lane

Supermann sagt:

Lois ist meine Freundin. Ich kenne sie schon seit zwei Wochen. Abends
besuche ich sie oft auf ihrem Balkon. Ich mag sie sehr gern und sie
findet mich Spitze! Manchmal fliegen wir zum Nordpol. Lois hat das sehr
gern. Ich bringe sie dann vor Mitternacht nach Hause, denn ich muß noch
zum Training. Ich schwimme dann 1000 Kilometer.
Am Wochenende kocht sie für mich. Ich sehe sie gern und oft – Klasse, nicht?

Lois schreibt in ihr Tagebuch:

Supermann ist mein Freund. Ich ...

_____

_____

_____

_____

_____

Fernsehen und Kino

 1. Programm

13.15 **Videotext für alle**
15.40 **Videotext für alle**
16.10 **Tagesschau**
16.15 Professor Grzimek. **Hermelin, Hase und andere Bundesrepublikaner**
17.00 **„Mensch, mach hinne . . ."** Jörg und sein Praktikum. Aus der Sendereihe „Denkste!? Jörg ist begeistert. Sein Lehrer hat ihm eine Praktikumsstelle in einer Autowerkstatt besorgt. Es stehen Jörg also vier interessante Wochen in seinem Traumberuf bevor. Und: die Schule fällt auch aus. Doch der erste Kontakt mit der Berufswelt ist für Jörg sehr ernüchternd. Nur mit Mühe vermag er die Monotonie des Arbeitsalltags zu überstehen. Einige Kollegen nutzen seine Unwissenheit aus. Es gibt eine Menge Ärger.
17.50 **Tagesschau**
18.00 **Abendschau aktuell**
18.20 **Drei Damen vom Grill.** Wenn Oma eine Reise tut
18.50 **Abendschau**
19.40 ARD-Sport extra. **Fußball-Länderspiel: England – Bundesrepublik Deutschland.** In der Halbzeitpause gegen 20.30: **Tagesschau**
21.30 **Titel, Thesen, Temperamente.** Kulturmagazin
22.30 **Tagesthemen**
23.00 **Atomstrom um jeden Preis?** Die Zukunft der Kernenergie. Von Klaus Ullrich und Josef Turecek
23.45 **Tagesschau**

 2. Programm

13.15 **Videotext für alle**
15.40 **Videotext für alle**
15.57 **ZDF – Ihr Programm**
16.00 **Heute**
16.04 **Moritz lernt schwimmen**
16.35 **Die verlorenen Inseln**
17.00 **Heute**
17.08 **Tele-Illustrierte**
18.05 **Raumschiff Enterprise**
18.57 **ZDF – Ihr Programm**
19.00 **Heute**
19.30 **Der internationale Jugendfilm: Achtung Rotlicht!** (Kanada – 1980). Der bekannte Fernsehjournalist Peter Lyon beschäftigt sich in seinen Sendungen mit harten Themen aus dem sozialen Bereich: Bauskandale, Jugendarbeitslosigkeit, Jugendvandalismus. Dabei steht er unter ständigem Druck seiner Fernsehstation, die von ihm möglichst hohe Einschaltzahlen fordert. Bei der intensiven Arbeit an einem Bericht über randalierende Jugendliche in einer Vorstadtsiedlung entgeht ihm völlig, daß sein eigener Sohn Kevin sich der Jugendbande angeschlossen hat.
20.15 **Bilanz**
21.00 **Heute-Journal**
21.20 **Mittwochslotto – 7 aus 38**
21.25 **Die Straßen von San Francisco**
22.10 **Das geht Sie an**
22.15 **„Der Verstand ist ein lästiger Narr . . ."** Teresa von Avila
22.45 **Die Rückkehrer.** Ehemalige Auswanderer berichten
23.15 **Heute**

This evening's TV programmes:

- *Is there anything for sports fans?*
- *What do they call the regular news programmes on Channel 1?*
- *Channel 2 has two popular series from America, one about space and one about the battle against crime. Can you recognise them from their titles here? What do we call them in English?*
- *Can you work out what any of the other programmes might be about?*

---

3. PROGRAMM 26. Juli DI

22.35 **Dallas** - Die Erbin

Alan Beam (Randolph Powell) möchte Lucy (Charlene Tilton, r.) heiraten und drängt sie, mit ihm Ringe auszusuchen. Doch Lucy hat es damit nicht so eilig

ATLANTIK Telefon 55 56 70 Ecke Sonnen- Schwanthalerstr. **Kino 1** 12.40, 15.00, 17.20, 20.20 ab 16 Jahren

Ein Film wie ein Erdbeben, ein Mann wie ein Vulkan! CONAN DER BARBAR

ATLANTIK Telefon 55 56 70 Ecke Sonnen- Schwanthalerstr. **Kino 2** 13.30, 16.45, 20.00 Uhr ab 16 Jahren

Henry Fonda Jason Robards
Charles Bronson Claudia Cardinale

Spiel mir das Lied vom Tod

▲
◀ *Are you old enough to be allowed in to see these films?*

◀ *What sort of film is showing on screen 3 at the Stachus Center?*

STACHUS-KINO-CENTER
KINO 4 9.15, S. ab 11.15, 13.15, 15.15, 17.15, 19.15, 21.15 – 16 J.

Die unheimlichen Visionen des **NOSTRADAMUS** sind von bedrückender Aktualität!
2. Woche !!!

Die Prophezeiung des NOSTRADAMUS
WELTKATASTROPHE 1999
Dieser Film zeigt in schrecklichem Realismus, was unserer Erde in naher Zukunft bevorsteht, wenn die Prophezeiung eintrifft.

Der Countdown läuft – es ist schon fünf vor zwölf! Die Zukunft beginnt!

STACHUS-KINO-CENTER
KINO 3 10.00, 12.00, 14.00, 16.00, 18.00, 20.00, 22.00, ab 16 J.

Der erste chinesische Seeräuber-Film
Gewaltig wie ein Orkan

Die Teufelspiraten von KAU-LUN
TI LUNG · DAVID CHIANG
FAN MEI SHENG · WANG KUANG YU
Regie CHANG CHEH

What sort of audience would you expect to see at the Walt Disney film?
What does the poster tell us about the film?
▶

WALT DISNEY'S Zeichentrickfilm-Klassiker
Ein Kinospaß für die ganze Familie
WALT DISNEY PRODUCTIONS **2. Woche**

SUSI und STROLCH

EINE HUNDELIEBE MIT HAPPY-END

TECHNICOLOR
© Walt Disney Productions MCMLXXXII

KARLSTOR Neuhauser Str. 34, Tel. 55 42 00 Kino 1: 13 - 15 - 17 - 19 - 21 Uhr

ROYAL am Goetheplatz · Telefon 53 39 56/57 Kino E: 13 - 15 - 17 - 19 - 21 Uhr

Ü1 **Schreibe einen Dialog** *(The responses below will help you.)*

o *Do you speak English?* • _____

_____

o _____ • _____

_____

o _____ • _____

o _____

_____ • _____

_____

o _____ • _____

| Nach Wien. | Ja, stimmt. Ich will nach Zürich. | Hast du einen Stadtplan von München? |

Ja, aber ich spreche hier lieber deutsch.

Aus Toronto. Wohin willst du?

Du kommst wohl aus England?

Fein, danke!

Gut, woher kommst du?

Hier, da ist er.

Ü2 **Bitte fragen**

o _____ ? • Aus Brighton.

o _____ ? • Nach Wien.

o _____ ? • Seit zwei Wochen.

o _____ ? • Schwimmen? Ja, prima.

Ü3 **Was sagt man in folgenden Situationen?**

a) *Imagine you are in a German town and you want to ask someone the way to the station:*

Entschuldigen Sie, _____

b) *Now you explain to someone the way to the post office:*

Zur Post? _____

(go straight on and then first left)

Ü4 **Nach dem Weg fragen**

Three different ways of asking the way:

1. Entschuldigung, wo _____

2. Bitte, wie _____

3. Entschuldigung, gibt _____

KAUFHAUS
RATHAUS
TELEFONZELLE

Ü5

Orientierung in der Stadt

Was sagen die Leute?

Schreibe Fragen und Antworten

STADION
KAUFHAUS
Post
BAHNHOF
BANK
TAXI
Polizei
POLIZEI
Kaiserstr.
Bahnhofsplatz
Bahnhofstr.
RATHAUS
Wald-weg
Stadt Schwimmbad
Rathausplatz
Badstr. E
Jugendzentrum
Schulstr.
Ringstr.
Markt Str.
Goethe-Str.
SELBST TANKEN
SCHULE

Bitte, _____
Zum Bahnhof?

Sie _____
Kaiserstraße
Dann
Rechts   E
der Bahnhofsplat

G
?

Ein Schwimmbad?

Wo ist das Jugend-
zentrum?

Also hier
Dann

Ü6 Wie komme ich zum?
zur?

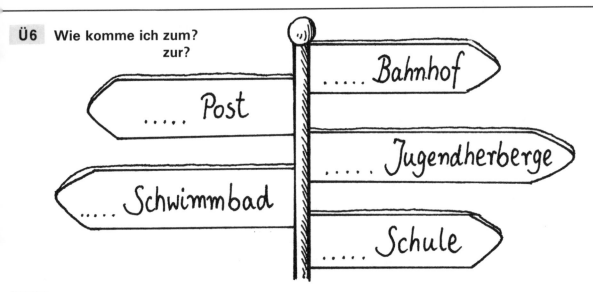

..... Bahnhof

..... Post

..... Jugendherberge

Schwimmbad .....

..... Schule

Ü7 **Das Stadtzentrum von München. Bitte den Weg erklären:**

Giving directions:

a) Vom Hauptbahnhof ⟶ zum Karolinenplatz (31)

b) Vom Marienplatz (8) ⟶ zum Hofbräuhaus (17)

c) Vom Odeonsplatz (23) ⟶ zum Nationaltheater (21)

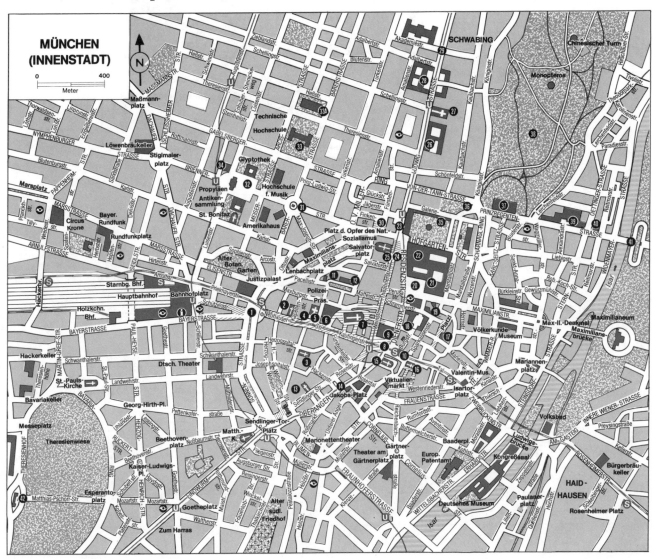

Ü8 Wie kommt man zur Burg Schwaneck?

Finding your way to Burg Schwaneck, a youth hostel, in Pullach, south of Munich.

Übersicht über Verkehrs-verbindungen:	1. Abfahrt letzte Abfahrt		Hauptverkehrs-zeiten morgens und abends	übrige Tageszeiten	Endstation
S 10 ab Mü.-Holz-kirchner-Bhf.	**5.09 Uhr** **23.39 Uhr**		zu jeder vollen und halben Stunde	zu jeder halben Stunde	Bahnhof Pullach
Bus 62 u. 162 ab U-Bahn-Station Harras	Bus 62 **6.02** **0.52**	Bus 162 **5.32** **19.12**	**alle 20** Minuten	**alle 30** Minuten	Haltestelle Pater-Rupert-Mayer-Straße Pullach

Von den Haltestellen der Busse bzw. vom Bahnhof ist die Burg zu Fuß in knapp 10 Minuten zu erreichen.

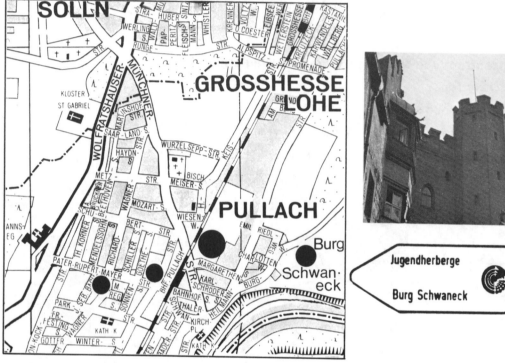

Look for the following information:

1. *How often does a bus arrive in Pullach during daytime?*

   _____

2. *When does the last train (S-Bahn) leave Holzkirchner Bahnhof, a station in Munich?*

   _____

3. *How long does it take to walk to the youth hostel from the station?*

   _____

4. *Write down the names of the streets you would have to go along.*

   _____, _____

   _____, _____

Jugendherberge Burg Schwaneck
Diese Jugendherberge ist nur
12 km vom Stadtzentrum ent-
fernt. Kann auch mit der
S-Bahn erreicht werden.
Sportplätze.
Burgweg 4-6, 8023 Pullach
Tel. 7 93 06 43
Anreise: S 1 bis Pullach.
Preise pro Person inklusive
Frühstück und Bettwäsche:
im 6-Bett-Zimmer: 9.20 DM
im 4-Bett-Zimmer: 10.20 DM
im 3- und 4-Bett-Zimmer 15 DM
im Doppelzimmer: 17 DM
im Einzelzimmer: 20 DM
Warme Mahlzeit 5.80 DM
Kalte Mahlzeit 4.80 DM
7 bis 23.30 Uhr

Ü9 Bitte den Text lesen

1. *Can you find out how far away Pullach is from Munich?*

   _____

2. *How much would it cost to stay in a three-bedded room? What would that be in your currency?*

   _____

3. *Would you be able to get a hot meal at 7 p.m.?*

   _____ *because* _____

4. *Write down the address of the youth hostel:*

   _____

   What do the numbers mean? Ask your teacher if you don't know.

Ü10 **Bitte die Texte A und B lesen**

A Trampen ist <u>billig</u>. Darum reisen viele
Jungen und Mädchen in den Ferien mit dem
Daumen. Außerdem trifft man neue Freunde,
wenn man an der Straße steht.
Tramper müssen sich gut vorbereiten. Ein
<u>Schlafsack</u>, eine Karte und Geld zum Über-
nachten gehören ins <u>Gepäck</u>. Und noch einige Regeln: Kein Autostop auf Autobahnen,
nicht nachts und nicht allein trampen.

B **Kontakte**

Work Camps (gemeinsame Arbeit) und Sozialdienste, Internationale Studienseminare,
Deutsche Sprachkurse, Stu-
dienreisen und Wanderungen,
Internationale Ferientreffen,
Aufenthalte in deutschen Fa-
milien: über dies alles infor-
miert die Broschüre „<u>Interna-
tionale Begegnungen</u>", heraus-
gegeben vom „Studienkreis für
Tourismus e. V.", Dampf-
schiffstraße 2, 8130 Starnberg.

A 1. *Find out what the underlined words mean.*

_____

2. *Can you now give two reasons why hitchhiking is so popular among
young people?*

_____

3. *What should you take with you as a must?*

_____

4. *Mention two things one ought to avoid when hitchhiking.*

_____

Nun auf deutsch antworten

5. Warum macht Trampen Spaß?

_____

6. Was soll man mitnehmen?

_____

7. Was ist nicht so gut beim Trampen?

_____

B 1. *The key words in this text are "Internationale Begegnungen".
They are the title of a brochure. Find out what 'Begegnungen' (= Treffen)
means.*

2. *Now read the text again. Try to work out what kind of information you
would get from the brochure if you ordered it from the address in
Starnberg (Bavaria).*

Ü11 **Taxi!!!**

der Marktplatz	⟶	Zum Marktplatz, bitte!
das Schwimmbad	⟶	Zum Schwimmbad, bitte!
die Post	⟶	Zur Post, bitte!

Taxi!	⟶	Bahnhof bitte!	(der Bahnhof)
Taxi!	⟶	Marktstraße bitte!	(die Straße)
Taxi!	⟶	Rathaus bitte!	(das Rathaus)
Taxi!	⟶	Bank bitte!	(die Bank)
Taxi!	⟶	Stadion bitte!	(das Stadion)

Ü12 **Entschuldigung! Wie ...?**

Excuse me, please!
How far is it? How do I get there?

1. Wie weit ist es bis ⟶ Bahnhof? – Etwa 200 Meter.

2. Wie komme ich ⟶ Bank? – Geradeaus bis ⟶ Kreuzung und dann rechts bis ⟶ Bank.

3. Wie komme ich ⟶ Rathaus? – Hier geradeaus und dann rechts.

4. Wie komme ich ⟶ Touristen-Information? – Sie gehen hier links bis ⟶ Rathausplatz und dann nach links.

5. Wie komme ich ⟶ Bahnhof? – Hier geradeaus bis ⟶ Bahnhofstraße und dann links.

Ü13 **Wo ist das?**

Where are these places?
(look at p. 68 in the course book)

 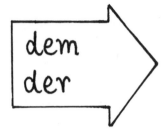 

1. Das Kaufhaus ist _____

2. Der Briefkasten ist _____

3. Das Jugendzentrum ist _____

4. Die Bank ist _____

5. Die Haltestelle ist _____

Ü14 **Bitte ergänzen**

Now complete the answers to these questions:

1. Gibt es hier ein Jugendzentrum?   – Ja, (in) _____ Marktstraße.

2. Wo finde ich hier eine Telefonzelle?   – (An) _____ Park.

3. Ist hier eine Bushaltestelle?   – Ja, (neben) _____ Schule.

4. Wo finde ich ein Taxi?   – (Auf) _____ Bahnhofsplatz.

5. Gibt es hier eine Disco?   – Ja, (in) _____ Jugendzentrum.

6. Wo finde ich hier eine Bank?   – (Bei) _____ Bahnhof.

Ü15 Kannst du helfen?

Entschuldigung, wo ist bitte das Rathaus?

_____

Wo ist hier eine Bank?

_____

Entschuldigung, wo ist hier die Post?

_____

Entschuldigung, wo ist hier das Schwimmbad?

_____

Wo ist hier bitte eine Telefonzelle?

_____

Wie komme ich am besten zum Bahnhof?

_____

Ü16 Bitte ausfüllen

_Fill in the days
and/or the dates in this letter._

25	Fr		
26	Sa		
27	So	Palmsonntag	
28	Mo	*nach London*	13
29	Di	"	
30	Mi	" *nach Edinburgh*	
31	Do	"	

APRIL 1983

1	Fr	Karfreitag	*Edinburgh*	
2	Sa		*nach London*	
3	So	Ostersonntag	*Canterbury*	
4	Mo	Ostermontag	*Windsor*	14
5	Di		*nach Deutschland*	
6	Mi			
7	Do		*Schule !! Oh Gott!*	
8	Fr			
9	Sa			
10	So			

23.3.

Lieber Andi,
nächste Woche macht unsere Klasse eine
Osterreise nach England. Am _____
und am _____ sehen wir uns
London an. Wir fahren dann nach
Schottland und sind am _____ , am
_____ und am _____ in Edinburgh.
Am _____ fahren wir dann nach London
zurück und besuchen am _____
Canterbury. Wir sind am _____ in
Windsor. Am _____ geht's
dann in der Schule wieder los! Soll ich
Dir etwas aus England mitbringen?
    Bitte schreibe schnell!
        Viele Grüße
        Wolfgang

Travel

Holidays, cheap flights, special offers for young people - could you explain to a friend what is being advertised here?

On which days of the week are the cheap flights to London and to which airport do they fly?

How about a cruise - what would you see?

Is there any age limit on cheap rail travel with Transalpino?

How much can you save?

How can you travel to Berlin?

DB Die Bahn

Mit dem Flugzeug

Mit dem Bus

Mit dem Auto

ALLE WEGE NACH BERLIN

Mit der Bahn

Ü1 Kleine Dialoge. Was fehlt hier?

1. o _____ du auch Moped fahren?

   ● Nein, aber ich _____ es lernen.

2. o Wo ist das Jugendzentrum?

   ● Da drüben, wir _____ geradeaus gehen.

3. o Peter _____ in den Ferien nach England trampen.

   ● Mit 14? _____ er das denn?

   o Er trampt ja nicht allein.

4. o _____ ich mal telefonieren?

   ● Ja, gern.

Ü2

Und am Samstag eine Party!

Complete this conversation.

o Was _____ wir machen? Hast du eine Idee?

● Moment, _____ ich mal ein Papier haben?

  Ich _____ eine Liste machen.

o Hier, du _____ in mein Heft schreiben.

● Also, wer kommt?

o Klaus, Gabi, Ute und Norbert _____ kommen.

  Peter _____ leider nicht. Er _____ zum

  Handballtraining.

● Schade! Er _____ so gut Gitarre spielen.

o Macht nichts! Wir _____ meinen Plattenspieler

  nehmen. Und Klaus und Ute _____ neue Platten

  kaufen.

● Vielleicht _____ ich unsere Filmkamera

  mitbringen. Ich _____ meinen Vater mal fragen.

o Und am Freitag _____ Gabi und Norbert

  einkaufen: Cola, Limonade und Chips.

● Alles klar.

Now practise this conversation with your partner.

Ü3 **Dialoge zum Üben**

Practise these short conversations. (Use the words in the margin, too.)

a) o Willst du wirklich dein <u>Moped</u> reparieren?

    ● Ja, das will ich.

    o Und das kannst du ganz allein?

    ● Natürlich kann ich das.   o Ich weiß noch nicht.

       Ich muß nur Zeit haben.   Ja, nur kaputtmachen darf ich es nicht.

                        Und weiter ...

das Radio

der Plattenspieler

b) o Du, Gabi, ich _____ gern <u>deine Gitarre</u> haben!

    ● Das geht nicht.

    o Warum _____ ich <u>sie</u> nicht haben?

    ● Heute spiele ich. Du _____ <u>sie</u> morgen haben.

    o Dann nicht.

der Fußball

das Fahrrad

c) o Peter, _____ du am Samstag zur Party kommen?

    ● Am Samstag _____ ich leider nicht.

    o Und warum nicht? _____ du zu Hause helfen?

    ● Nein, ich _____ mein Radio reparieren.

    o Mach das doch morgen.

    ● Geht nicht. Keine Zeit.

    o Das find ich aber blöd.

    ● Ach was.

Bitte noch zwei Dialoge schreiben

Use the same framework as in c, but change the activities.

Ü4 **Was bedeuten die Symbole 1–10?**

What do the signs 1-10 mean?

München Hauptbahnhof

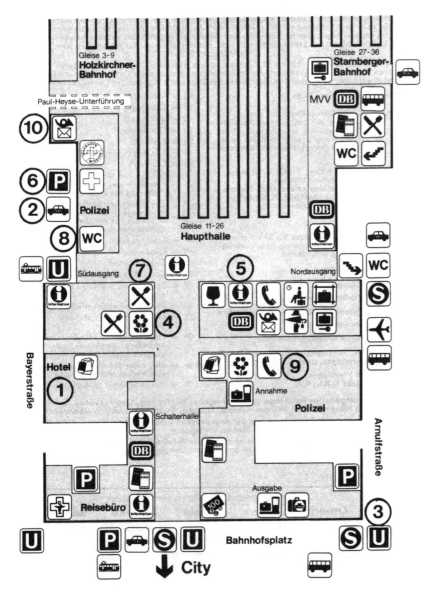

Match each number in the diagram with the correct expression below.

Hier kann man .....

9 telefonieren

___ auf ein Taxi warten

___ Informationen bekommen

___ ein Hotel buchen

___ mit der U-Bahn fahren

___ Briefmarken kaufen

___ auf die Toilette gehen

___ parken

___ etwas essen

___ Blumen kaufen

Ü5 **Bitte ergänzen: müssen – können – wollen – dürfen – sollen**

Now complete these sentences with the help of exercise 4.

1 : Wir _____

2 : Taxi? Sie _____ hier _____

3 : Du _____

4 : S_____ ich _____ ?

5 : Hier _____ ihr _____

6 : _____ _____ nur hier _____ .

7 : Da _____ man _____

8 : _____ du _____ ?

9 : Moment, ich _____ schnell _____

10 : _____

Ü6 Was bedeuten die Verkehrszeichen?

What do the traffic signs mean?

Hier _____

Hier _____

Fußgänger _____

Autos _____

Man _____

Bei Rot _____

Ü7 **Diesen Text bitte lesen**

Wichtige Punkte aus dem Gesetz zur Jugendarbeit*

(= Jugendarbeitsschutzgesetz)

- Das Mindestalter für eine Arbeit ist 15 Jahre.
- Kinderarbeit ist nur für Kinder über 13 Jahre möglich, und zwar in der Landwirtschaft bis 3 Stunden täglich, Zeitungen ins Haus bringen oder beim Sport helfen bis 2 Stunden.
- Der Urlaub (= Ferien) dauert 25 bis 30 Tage.
- In der Woche sollen Jugendliche nicht mehr als 4o Stunden arbeiten.
- Eine Arbeitswoche hat 5 Tage. Am Wochenende und an Feiertagen ist frei.
- Vor 8 Uhr dürfen Kinder nicht mit der Arbeit beginnen.

Bitte ausfüllen

Arbeiten? Aber ..... was steht im Text?

	Wie alt?	Wann?	Wie lange?	Was?
Arbeit →				
Kinderarbeit →				
Beginn der Arbeit →				
Wie viele Tage pro Woche? →				
Wie viele Stunden pro Woche? →				
Und für Kinder? →				
Arbeiten für Kinder? →				
Ferien? →				

* There are laws which control the employment of young people and protect their rights.

Ü8 **Nun diesen Text lesen**

Jeden Morgen und Mittag, wenn die Schule beginnt und wenn sie zu Ende ist, stehen an Fußgängerüberwegen in der Bundesrepublik rund 60 000 Schülerlotsen. Sie bringen ihre Mitschüler sicher über die Straße. Die Schülerlotsen gibt es seit 30 Jahren. In dieser Zeit hatte kein Kind an den Übergängen einen Unfall.

1. *What would* <u>Schülerlotsen</u> *be in English?*

2. *What is their job?*

3. *Who acts as Schülerlotse in Germany?*

4. *Find out what* <u>Unfall</u> *means.*

   Can you now work out the meaning of the last sentence?

Ü9 **Verkehrszeichen**

- *Try to explain these traffic signs to a German friend.*
  Match the signs with the right explanation.

a
School crossing patrol

b
Maximum speed

c
Keep left

d
STOP 100 yds
Distance to "Stop" line ahead

e
During every working day

Mon-Sat 8 am-6·30 pm

f
Bus lane

1. Man muß links fahren.
2. Busse sollen hier fahren.
3. Hier wollen Kinder über die Straße gehen.
4. Nach ___m müssen alle halten.
5. Von Montag bis Samstag darf man hier von 8 Uhr bis 18.30 Uhr nicht parken.
6. Man darf nur _____ km fahren.

a					
3					

Ü10

Was kann man hier tun? *Write it down in short.*

1. _____ 2. _____

3. _____ 4. _____

Ü11 **Bitte die Verben einsetzen**

„Komm, wir gehen schwimmen!"

Klaus und Bertram _____ schwimmen gehen. Sie _____ zu Max

und sagen: o "Komm, wir _____ schwimmen, das Wasser hat heute schon

21 Grad." Max _____ : ● "Es _____ jetzt noch nicht, ich _____

erst meine Hausaufgaben fertigmachen. Vielleicht _____ ich danach ins

Schwimmbad." - o "Die Hausaufgaben _____ du heute abend machen." - ● "Heute

abend _____ ich Maria helfen. Sie schreibt morgen eine Klassenarbeit. " -

o "Das _____ zu lange. Bring deine Schulsachen mit! Wir _____

bis fünf Uhr schwimmen, und dann kommst du mit zu uns. Wir haben unsere Hausaufgaben

schon fertig und _____ dir helfen. Am Abend _____ du dann nach

Hause _____ und Maria helfen." - ● "Gut, ich _____ mit."

sagt   gehen   können   muß   kommen   wollen   kannst

komme   kannst   können   dauert   geht   gehen   komme

muß

Ü12 **Verbformen schreiben** ─────────────────────────────

Complete these sentences with the correct form of the verbs.

dürfen	**müssen**
What you are allowed to do (or not!)	*What you <u>must</u> do.*

In der Schule _____ ich in der Pause Fußball spielen.

_____ wir nicht rauchen.

_____ wir immer viele Aufgaben machen.

_____ man viel lernen.

Der Lehrer sagt: "Ihr _____ hier nicht spielen!"

"Du _____ fleißiger arbeiten!"

Ü13 **Verbformen schreiben**

Complete these sentences with the correct form of the verb können.

können

Was man in Deutschland machen kann...

Wir _____ junge Leute treffen.

Du _____ viel Deutsch sprechen.

Ihr _____ in Jugendherbergen übernachten.

Man _____ aber auch auf einen Campingplatz gehen.

Im Schwarzwald, im Harz und in den Alpen _____ man prima

skifahren.

Auf vielen Seen _____ man segeln.

Wir _____ Ferien auf einem Bauernhof machen.

Ü14 **wollen** **können**

Complete this conversation.

o Was _____ ihr machen?

● Wir _____ Fußball spielen.

o Gabi auch?

● Ja, sie _____ auch spielen.

o Blödsinn! Ein Mädchen _____ nicht Fußball spielen!

● Doch! Gabi _____ sehr gut spielen.

o Stimmt das Gabi? _____ du auch spielen? Oder _____

du was anderes machen?

● Nein, nein. Los, wir spielen!

Ü15 sollen

Was soll ein guter Schüler ⎱
           eine gute Schülerin ⎰ machen?

What should a good pupil do?

Er/Sie _____ viele Hausaufgaben _____.

Man _____ viele Bücher _____.

Er/Sie _____ fleißig _____.

Die Schüler _____ freundlich zu den Lehrern _____.

_____ ich ihr Heft immer _____? Aber natürlich!

So ein Schüler _____ lieber zu Hause _____!

Wieviel Hausaufgaben?

Ü16 Beantworte die Fragen

Answer these questions in your exercise book:

Was kannst du gut - und was nicht so gut?

Was willst du am Wochenende machen - und was nicht?

Und die Eltern - Was sagen sie dazu?

Was darfst du mit sechzehn?

Was darfst du in der Schule nicht machen?

Wann mußt du in der Schule sein?

Ü17 Eltern *Parents*

Bitte ergänzen: wollen – dürfen – können – müssen – sollen

"Mutti, _____ ich heute abend ins Kino gehen? Warum _____

ich Klaus immer mitnehmen, er ist zu jung! Mein Freund Martin _____

auch mitkommen. Wir _____ Klaus nicht mitnehmen. Er _____ zu

Hause Musik hören. Mit so einem kleinen Kind _____ man nichts machen.

Ich _____ also ohne Klaus nicht weggehen? Na gut. Er _____

mitkommen. Diesmal!"

Ü1 **Informiere über dein Land**

London

Beispiel:

In *Großbritannien* leben _____ Millionen Menschen.

Großbritannien, das sind _____,

_____ und *Schottland*.

Die Sprache ist _____. In *Wales* spricht

man auch _____.

_____ ist _____ qkm groß.

Die Hauptstadt ist _____.

Ü2 **Nun informiere über deine Familie**

Was kannst du schreiben und sagen?

Vorname:
Alter:
Größe:
Beruf:
Hobbys:

Ich

meine Mutter

mein Vater

meine Schwester

mein Bruder

Abfahrt Kassel

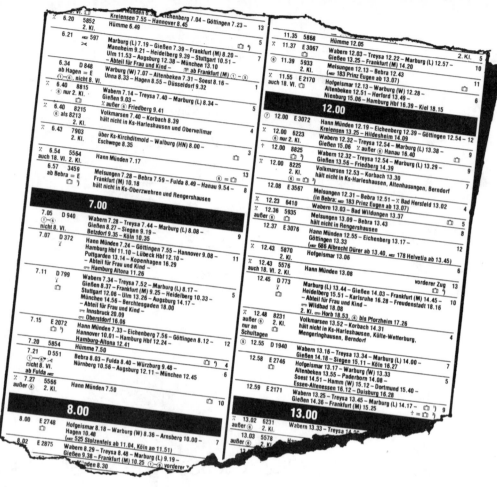

Ü3 Bitte einsetzen

1. Klaus muß um 12 Uhr in Hamburg sein. Er muß um _____ in Kassel abfahren.

2. Beatrix muß um 10 Uhr in Heidelberg sein. Sie muß in Kassel um _____ abfahren.

3. Alex fährt um 12.37 in Kassel ab. Er ist um _____ in Göttingen.

4. Emine fährt um 11.39 nach Bebra. Um _____ hält der Zug in Melsungen.

5. Sven fährt um _____ in Kassel ab und ist um 16.29 in Kopenhagen.

6. Herr Kaufmann nimmt den Zug um 6.21 ab Kassel. Um _____ ist er in Stuttgart.

7. Bettina möchte um 14 Uhr in Marburg sein. Sie kann in Kassel um _____ oder um _____ abfahren.

8. Fred fährt in Kassel um _____ ab und ist um 14.45 in Frankfurt.

Zeichenerklärung:

✝	= an Sonntagen und allgemeinen Feiertage... Als allgemeine Feiertage im Bundesgebiet gelten: Neujahr, Karfreitag, Ostermontag, 1. Mai, Christi Himmelfahrt, Pfingstmontag, 17. Juni, Bußtag, 1. und 2. Weihnachtstag.	①	= Montag
		②	= Dienstag
		③	= Mittwoch
		④	= Donnerstag
✗	= an Werktagen [Am 18. VI. Verkehr wie ✝]	⑤	= Freitag
außer ⑤	= täglich außer samstags	⑥	= Samstag
✗ außer ⑤	= werktags außer samstags	⑦	= Sonntag
✝ vor ✗	= an Sonn- und Feiertagen vor Werktagen		Züge mit dieser Angabe der Wochentage verkehren, auch, wenn der betreffende Tag auf einen Feiertag fällt

Ü4 Reisen *Travelling*

Which piece of luggage belongs to each of the travellers?

a	
b	
c	
d	
e	

① das Fernglas

der Kinderwagen ③

⑤ der Rucksack

② die Tasche

④ der Koffer

Ü5 Wie heißt das auf deutsch?

Ü6   Was bedeuten diese Wörter?

schön

frech

stark

Wie sind deine Klassenkameraden

superfleißig

lustig

schüchtern

sportlich

(Look up the words and others you
might want to use).
How would you describe your own
classmates?

John ist ....

1 Deine Hobbys

Ich heiße .... und bin ....
Meine Hobbys sind ...

Und was noch?

2 Ein Telefondialog

Was sagen Claudia und Martin? *(Read this through first)*

C.: Hallo Martin,

    ... Party am ...

    ... du ...? ————————

                       M.: Ich ??????

                       Wann ...?

C.: ... halb ...

    ... Platten mitbringen?

                       M.: Na klar, ... tanzen

                       ... auch Gitarre ...?

C.: Nein, wir ...

    Aber vielleicht ...

                       M.: Also bis ...

                       Tschüs.

Schreibe den Dialog in dein Heft

3 Bitte den Brief ergänzen

Liebe Ulrike,

heute _____ ich aus Portsmouth in England. Dort

machen wir 3 Wochen _____ . Wir _____ in der

J_____e und _____ jeden Tag _____

Schwimmbad. Morgen _____ ich Richard. Er _____

sich sehr für _____ und _____ .

Tanzen _____ er langweilig. Am Freitag

_____ wir weiter nach Cornwall.

Bis bald.

*Herzliche Grüße
Deine Karin*

4 Was darf/kann/muß/soll man hier tun?

Autofahrer *k*_____ hier _____ und _____ .

Alle Autos *d*_____ hier nur 60 km _____ :

Fußgänger *s*_____ hier über die Straße _____ .

Peter *m*_____ _____ _____ .

Vater *d*_____ da _____ _____ waschen.

Ihr *s*_____ dort die _____ waschen.

Hier *k*_____ ihr
Post _____ _____ .

Man *d*_____ hier nicht Fahrrad fahren.

Cathy und John *k*_____ hier _____ .

Wir *m*_____ hier _____ .

5 Mache eine Liste: was du sollst – was du willst

Was ich soll / muß	Was ich will / möchte
Ich muß zu Hause immer helfen.	Ich will lieber mehr Zeit für mich haben.

6 Bitte ausfüllen

1. ○ _____ kommst du? – ● _____ München.

2. ○ _____ willst du? – ● _____ Barcelona.

3. ○ _____ ? – ● Seit drei Wochen.

7 Das Stadtzentrum von Berlin

Kannst du den Weg sagen?

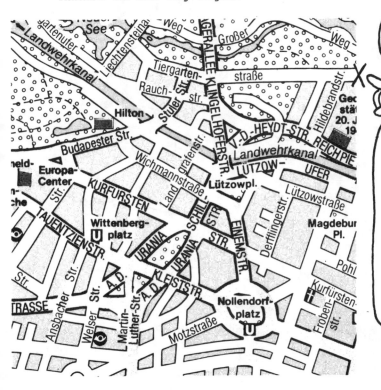

Entschuldigung, wie komme ich zum Europa-Center?

Zuerst hier . . . . .

8 **Was ist falsch? Unterstreiche die Wörter und schreibe den Text richtig**

JUTTA UND DIE CLIQUE

Sie hören zusammen viel _Sport_. In ihrer Freizeit trinken sie Cola. Am Wochenende fahren sie immer nach Hause. Abends müssen sie spätestens um 21.15 Uhr in der Disco sein. Jutta geht in die Disco putzen. Sie verdient dort 200 DM am Tag. Von dem Geld kauft sie sich meistens Platten. Morgens besucht sie gern ihren Freund.

Jeans oder Pullover
ins Geschäft   Tee   ~~Musik~~
  abends   im Monat
zu Hause   ins Grüne

Sie hören zusammen viel Musik.

_____
_____
_____
_____
_____
_____
_____
_____
_____

9 **Praktisch oder nicht?**

Postkarte

Viele Grüße aus Oberbayern!

Es geht mir: prima / ganz gut
Wetter: zu viel
Essen:
Jugendherberge: originell
Kennengelernt: 2 Mädchen / 1 Hund
Landschaft: grün
Heimweh: was ist das?
Euer Claude

An
Mama + Papa

Daheim

Zu Hause

Schreibe eine Postkarte auf Englisch.

(Find out what the underlined words mean.)

10 **So wünschen sich Schüler ihren Traumlehrer:**

lustig ✓
macht guten Unterricht ✓
verständnisvoll ✓
sieht einigermaßen aus ✓
kameradschaftlich ✓
nett, gutgelaunt ✓
gerecht ✓

Mein "Traumlehrer" sollte den Unterricht interessant machen.
Man sollte auch bei ihm etwas lernen. Außerdem sollten
die Tests nicht sehr schwer sein. Mein Lehrer sollte lustig sein,
jung, groß und schlank. Am liebsten ohne Bart. Mein Wunschlehrer
sollte viel Humor haben und die Fragen so beantworten, daß sie
für jeden klar sind.
Ich wünsche mir einen Lehrer, der viele Spiele und Ausflüge
macht. Ich finde, ein Lehrer sollte öfter Filme zeigen.

Eine Traumlehrerin sollte Zeit haben und mit den Schülern
Probleme besprechen. Aufgaben gibt sie wenig. Gut wäre es,
wenn sie mit uns über Noten und andere Sachen diskutieren
würde. Wichtig ist, daß sie die Schüler versteht. Sie darf
keine Lieblinge in der Klasse haben. Sie sollte Spaß verstehen
und alle Schüler wie normale Menschen behandeln und nicht wie
Babys.

a) Wie soll ein Traumlehrer sein?
Was steht im Text?
Suche 4 Adjektive

_____

b) Was ist auch wichtig (important)?
Schreibe 5 Alternativen

1. Der Lehrer _____

2. Er _____

3. _____

4. _____

5. _____

c) Was sagt dieser Text von einer Traumlehrerin?
Schreibe so viel wie möglich

Sie soll _____ (1)

_____ (2)

_____ (3)

_____ (4)

_____ (5)

d) Und _dein_ Traumlehrer?

_____

11 Bitte einsetzen

Rocky schwimmt gut.	+	Rocky hat Fußball gern. ♡	
Rocko schwimmt _____.	++	Er hat Volleyball _____. ♡♡	
Rockine schwimmt _____.	+++	Er hat Tischtennis _____. ♡♡♡	

12 Bitte einsetzen

1. Ich interessier_____ _____ für Fußball.

2. Bettina interessier_____ _____ für Marcus.

3. Wir interessier_____ _____ nicht für Mathe.

4. Interessier_____ du _____ auch für Fußball?

5. Thomas interessier_____ _____ für Musik.

13 Uhrzeiten schreiben

"Wann kommst du?"

9.00   Um neun!

12.50   _____

16.45   _____

17.30   _____

20.20   _____

14 Bitte antworten

"Entschuldigung, wo ist hier ein Briefkasten?"

1. neben/Kaufhaus
   Neben dem Kaufhaus

2. auf/Rathausplatz
   _____

3. in/Ringstraße
   _____

4. an/Jugendzentrum
   _____

5. in/Bahnhof
   _____

6. an/Schwimmbad
   _____

15   Bitte einsetzen:

a)   müssen: Wir _____ jetzt gehen.

Hier _____ du warten.

Ich _____ jetzt nach Hause.

Klaus _____ morgen in die Schule gehen.

b)   dürfen: Peter _____ Moped fahren.

Ich _____ am Samstag nicht in die Disco gehen.

_____ du bis 11 Uhr ausgehen?

Wir _____ am Sonntag nicht kommen.

c)   wollen: Was _____ du denn machen?

Ich _____ schnell zu Gabi.

Was _____ ihr?

Wir _____ ein Lied singen.

Was _____ Sie, mein Herr?

d)   können: _____ ich jetzt gehen?

Mein Freund _____ gut Deutsch.

_____ du fahren?

Gabi und ich _____ gut fahren.

_____ wir hier über die Straße gehen?

e)   sollen: Was _____ ich kaufen?

Du _____ nicht so viel arbeiten.

_____ wir den Plattenspieler mitbringen?

Was _____ die Schüler tun?

Der Lehrer _____ viele Hausaufgaben geben.

10 Landeskunde

Germany – The Federal Republic

As you already know there are several German-speaking countries. By far the largest is West Germany or, to give its proper name, the Federal Republic of Germany (Bundesrepublik Deutschland), which has a population of about 61 million people.

What does „Federal Republic" mean?

Firstly, it is a *Republic* - that means that it is headed by a President and not by a King or Queen. It is *Federal* because although it is divided into ten states (rather like the states in the U.S.A.) it acts as one country when it comes to such matters as postal services, railways, money, defence and foreign affairs.

The German for a *Federation*, where the States work together, is *Bund* - thus the name *Bundesrepublik*.

What do you think the following are?

Deutsche Bundespost	Bundespräsident
Deutsche Bundesbahn	Bundeskanzler
Bundesliga	Bundesbank

The Federal Republic is a democracy. The members of the Bundestag are elected every 4 years. The Bundestag is the Parliament. The members of the Bundestag elect the Bundeskanzler (Federal Chancellor) who is then the political leader of the country - rather like a British Prime Minister. However, the official Head of State is the Bundespräsident.

There is a written constitution called the *Grundgesetz* (Basic Law). The Federal Capital is Bonn, a medium-sized town which lies on the river Rhine.

The Federal Republic consists of ten States (Länder) plus West-Berlin.

Baden-Württemberg

Bayern

Bremen

Hamburg

Hessen

Niedersachsen

Nordrhein-Westfalen

Rheinland-Pfalz

Saarland

Schleswig-Holstein

Berlin (West)

The ten States each run their own Police and Education services. They also look after electricity, gas and water supplies. However, they do work together and so there are fewer differences than you might imagine. Here is a list in order of size of population.

Bundesrepublik Deutschland

	Millions
Nordrhein-Westfalen	17,0
Bayern	10,8
Baden-Württemberg	9,1
Niedersachsen	7,2
Hessen	5,5
Rheinland-Pfalz	3,6
Schleswig-Holstein	2,6
Hamburg	1,7
Saarland	1,1
Bremen	0,7
plus	
Berlin (West)	1,9

Each of these has a State Capital and a State Parliament (Landtag) also elected every four years. In Hamburg and Bremen the parliament is called the Bürgerschaft, in Berlin the Abgeordnetenhaus.

Can you find out?

1. *The capital city of each State (Landeshauptstadt)?*

2. *What have Hamburg and Bremen in common?*

3. *Several of the States have different names in English. Which are they?*

4. *What is special about Berlin?*

Quellennachweis für Texte und Abbildungen

Heinrich Bauer Vertriebs KG, Hamburg (S. 94 o.) aus: "Fernsehwoche" 30/38

Bildarchiv Huber, Garmisch-Partenkirchen (S. 42)

Deutsche Bundesbahn (S. 88) aus: "Ihr Zugbegleiter", April 1983; (107) Skizze aus "Taschenfahrplan Oberbayern", 1982/83; (116) Fahrplanauszug

Deutscher Sportbund, Frankfurt/Main (Hg.) (S. 80, 83) aus: Heft 21 "Aktion Trimm Dich"

FISA I. G., Palaudarias, 26 Barcelona (S. 41) Ansichtskarte

Frankfurter Societäts-Druckerei GmbH, Frankfurt am Main (S. 83, 84) Fotos aus: "Scala-Jugendmagazin" 2/82; (89, 90) aus Sonderheft 2/81; (100) Text aus: Heft 1/81

Fremdenverkehrsamt München (S. 91) Adressen aus: "München-Leitfaden für Jugendgruppen", 1982

Bjarne Geiges (S. 9, 25 u., 64 o. + u., 67 r., 119, 124) Fotos

Goethe-Institut, München (S. 94, 104) Anzeigen aus: W. Lohfert "Schule und Freizeit, Texte zur Landeskunde", 1982

Kreisjugendring München-Land (Hg.) (S. 5, 48, 98, 99) aus: Prospekt "Burg Schwaneck", 1978, Redaktion Helmuth Mayr, Pullach/Isartal

Volker Leitzbach (S. 10/11, 12, 13, 17, 18, 21, 25 o., 29, 34, 49, 63, 64 Mi., 67 l., 75, 81, 85, 89, 90, 105) Fotos

Fritz Mader (S. 127) Foto

Otto Versand, Hamburg (S. 30, 31) Ausrisse aus Katalog

Polyglott Verlag, München (S. 14, 97, 121) Kartenskizzen

Theo Scherling (S. 7, 38) Collagen

Statistisches Bundesamt, Wiesbaden (Hg.) (S. 127) Kartenskizze aus: "Zahlenkompaß", 1982, Verlag W. Kohlhammer

Süddeutscher Verlag, München (S. 84) Tabelle aus: "Abendzeitung", München

Angelika Sulzer (S. 36, 37, 61, 62, 68, 110) Fotos

Velber Verlag, Seelze (S. 77, 79, 91) Leserbriefe und Zeichnungen aus: "Treff" Schülermagazin, 1978; (113) Zeichnung "Hausaufgaben" aus Heft 2/83; (123) Text aus: Heft 9/82

Verlag Deutsches Jugendherbergswerk, Hauptverband für Jugendwandern und Jugendherbergen e. V., Detmold (S. 48) Auszug aus: "Deutsches Jugendherbergsverzeichnis 1983/84"

WEREK Pressebildagentur, München (S. 14, 15) Fotos

Focus on Grammar

1. Talking about yourself and other people

Ich bin 12.

Er heißt Herr Bieler.

Sie kommen aus Deutschland.

SINGULAR		ich
		du
		er es sie
PLURAL		sie

Words such as *I, you, he, she, they*, etc. are called PERSONAL PRONOUNS.

They tell us <u>who</u> we are talking about.

	sein	wohnen	kommen	heißen
ich	**bin**	wohn<u>e</u>	komm<u>e</u>	heiß<u>e</u>
du	<u>bist</u>	wohn<u>st</u>	komm<u>st</u>	heiß<u>t</u>
er es sie	<u>ist</u>	wohn<u>t</u>	komm<u>t</u>	heiß<u>t</u>
sie	<u>sind</u>	wohn<u>en</u>	komm<u>en</u>	heiß<u>en</u>

ß = SS

The words that tell us <u>what</u> these people <u>do</u> (or what they are) are called VERBS, for example:

⚠ sein = *to be*

wohnen = *to live*

kommen = *to come*

heißen = *to be called*

Notice that the last letters or "endings" on these verbs change when the PERSON changes.

How often does this happen with English verbs?

2. Making sentences

a) Asking questions

Wie	heißt	du?
Wie alt	bist	du?
Woher	kommst	du?
Wo	wohnst	du?
Wer	ist	das?
Wie alt	ist	er?
Wo	wohnen	sie?

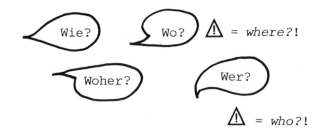

Wie? Wo? ⚠ = *where?!*

Woher? Wer?

⚠ = *who?!*

b) Answering questions or just making a statement

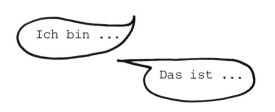

Ich bin ...

Das ist ...

Ich	heiße	Monika.
Ich	bin	zwölf.
Ich	komme	aus Deutschland.
Ich	wohne	in Kassel.
Das	ist	Klaus.
Er	ist	dreizehn.
Sie	wohnen	in Kassel.

3. "The"

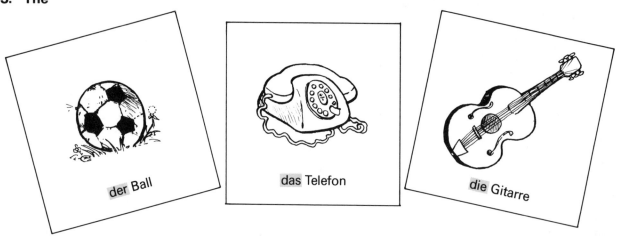

der Ball

das Telefon

die Gitarre

Note that there are 3 different words for THE!
More on this in Chapter 3.

Note also that in German <u>ALL NOUNS</u>* begin with a <u>capital letter</u>.

* Nouns are words for people or things.

4. "Mine" or "yours"? – Possessive pronouns (singular)

These words tell us <u>whose?</u>
Whose book? Whose teacher? etc.

Wo ist <u>mein</u> Paß?

Ist das <u>deine</u> Cassette?

Sabine ist <u>meine</u> Freundin.

Note: If it's a "die" word, add an -*e*:
mei<u>ne</u> Freundin, dei<u>ne</u> Gitarre

mein Ball · dein Ball

meine Gitarre · deine Gitarre

1. Speaking for yourself and others – Personal pronouns (plural)

Wir sind Freunde!

Wir wohnen in Holland.

Woher kommt ihr?

Wir kommen vom Mars.

	sein	wohnen	kommen	heißen
wir	sind	wohnen	kommen	heißen
ihr	seid	wohnt	kommt	heißt

Notice the endings on the
verbs when you are talking
about MORE THAN ONE person.

2. "Ours" or "yours"? – Possessive pronouns (plural)

unsere Gitarre   **eure** Gitarre

unser Ball   **euer** Ball

Notice that you add an -e if it's a "die" word.

⚠   <u>euer</u> - <u>eure</u>

Watch out for the spelling here.

3. Be polite!

○ Entschuldigung, sind Sie Herr Schulz?

● Nein, ich heiße Dracula.

(Notice that <u>Sie</u> has a capital <u>S</u> when it means *you*.

We have met 3 words for *you*:   du   ihr   Sie

Look at the way they are used in Chapter 2:

    du   -   another young person, a friend, a member of your family.

    ihr   -   more than one young person, friend etc. (*ihr* is the PLURAL of *du*)

    Sie   -   when speaking to an adult, especially someone you don't know.
            <u>Sie</u> is known as the <u>polite</u> <u>form</u> of *you*. It can also be plural.

Anyone under 16 years of age is automatically *du* - over 16 it gets more complicated!
When adults get to know one another very well they often change from *Sie* to *du*.

4. Making questions

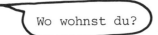

Wo wohnst du?

Wohnst du in Kassel?

We have already seen how you can ask questions by using such words as *Wie? Wer? Wo? Woher?* Another way is simply to put the verb first:

Wie	ist		Ihr Name?	Ist		Ihr Name	Steger?
Wie	heißen		Sie?	Heißen	Sie		Schulz?
Wer	sind		Sie?	Sind	Sie		Herr Schmidt?
Wie	heißt		du?	Heißt	du		Martin?
Wo	wohnst		du?	Wohnst	du		in Kassel?
Wer	ist		das?	Ist	das		Frau Schulz?

1. The definite and indefinite article

Nouns - people or things - usually come with "THE" (definite article) or "A" (indefinite article), e.g. _the house_ _a house_.

Think about the difference in meaning in the following two answers:

Was ist das?

Eine Tasche.

Die Tasche von Maria.

Which is definite, which is indefinite?

2. Gender – masculine, neuter, feminine

All nouns in German belong to one of these three groups. We can easily understand how _brother_ would be masculine and _sister_ would be feminine - but with "things" you have to be careful.

For example:

    der Fußball is a masculine noun
    das Auto is neuter
    die Tasche is feminine

(More in Lehrbuch 1, p. 33)

When you meet new words make a note or try to remember whether they are _der, das_ or _die_.

3. Plurals of nouns

	-e		¨e		-en		-n		--		-s
Tisch	-e	Stühl	¨e	Frau	-en	Tasche	-n	Lehrer	--	Kuli	-s
Bleistift	-e	Schwämm	¨e	Herr	-en	Schule	-n	Schüler	--	Cola	-s
Freund	-e	Fußbäll	¨e	Tourist	-en	Nummer	-n	Groschen	--		
Pfennig	-e					Klasse	-n	Mark	--		
Stück	-e		⚠	Landkarte	-n	Hamburger	--		
Schein	-e			Freundin-n-en		Schwester	-n				

Notice how many ways there are of making plurals in German.
How do we make plurals in English?

4. Two important verbs

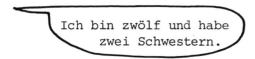

Ich bin zwölf und habe
zwei Schwestern.

The verbs *to be* and *to have* are important in any language.

Here they are in full:

				sein	haben
Singular		1. Person	ich	bin	habe
		2. Person	du	bist	hast
			Sie	sind	haben
		3. Person	er/es/sie	ist	hat
Plural		1. Person	wir	sind	haben
		2. Person	ihr	seid	habt
			Sie	sind	haben
		3. Person	sie	sind	haben

1. Subject and object

Hast du einen Kuli?

Ja, nimm den.

Notice the two "new" words *einen* and *den*. Why do we need them? We have already seen (in Chapter 3) that it is *der Kuli* or *ein Kuli*, so why the change?

Let us look at English first:

> Martin doesn't like the teacher.

Now replace one of the underlined words by *he*.
- *He* (Martin) doesn't like the teacher.

Now replace something else by *him*.
- Martin doesn't like *him* (the teacher).

We know, because we have used it so many times, when to put *he* and when to put *him*. If we were to explain what we were doing we could say that *he* (Martin) is the subject because *he* is the one who dislikes the teacher, whereas the teacher is the object because it is happening to *him*.

In German you have to do this not only with pronouns (*I/me, he/him, she/her*, etc.) but also with nouns and the articles with them:

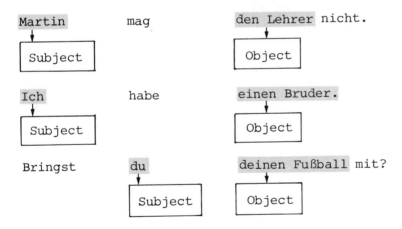

Notice that *mein, dein, unser*, etc. can change also.

When we look at how language works we use technical names to describe what is happening - just as we do in science. When a noun or pronoun is the subject we say it is in the NOMINATIVE CASE and when it is the object we say it is in the ACCUSATIVE CASE.

In German you will notice that it is only the <u>Masculine form</u> (*der, ein, mein, dein,* etc.) which changes from Nominative to Accusative:

Nominativ	Das	ist	das	Heft.	Neutrum
Akkusativ	ich	habe	das	Heft.	
Nominativ	Das	ist	die	Tasche.	Femininum
Akkusativ	Thomas	nimmt	die	Tasche.	
Nominativ	Das	ist	der	Kuli.	Maskulinum
Akkusativ	Thomas	nimmt	den	Kuli.	

Nominativ	Hier	ist	ein	Heft.	Neutrum
Akkusativ	Danke,	ich habe	ein	Heft.	
Nominativ	Das	ist	eine	Tasche.	Femininum
Akkusativ	Danke,	ich habe	eine	Tasche.	
Nominativ	Hier	ist	ein	Kuli.	Maskulinum
Akkusativ	Ich	habe	einen	Kuli.	

2. "Ein" – "kein"

ein	-	kein
eine	-	keine
einen	-	keinen

ein Buch

kein Buch

Bringt ihr eure Gitarre mit?

Nein, wir haben doch keine Gitarre.

Notice how *kein* is used for saying what you don't have. In German you don't normally say *nicht ein* but *kein*.

3. Verbs which separate

<u>Nehmt</u> bitte die Hausaufgaben <u>heraus</u>!

Wir gehen schwimmen. <u>Kommst</u> du <u>mit</u>?

This is very similar to the way in which we add extra information to ordinary verbs in English:

Take your books <u>out</u>!
Are you coming <u>with</u> us?

In German the extra word goes to the end:

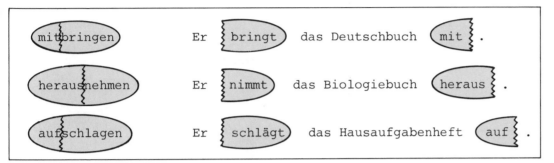

mitbringen	Er bringt das Deutschbuch mit .
herausnehmen	Er nimmt das Biologiebuch heraus .
aufschlagen	Er schlägt das Hausaufgabenheft auf .

Here are two of these separable verbs in full:

ich	nehme	.....	heraus
du	nimmst	.....	heraus
er es sie	nimmt	.....	heraus
wir	nehmen	.....	heraus
ihr	nehmt	.....	heraus
sie	nehmen	.....	heraus

ich	schlage	.....	auf
du	schlägst	.....	auf
er es sie	schlägt	.....	auf
wir	schlagen	.....	auf
ihr	schlagt	.....	auf
sie	schlagen	.....	auf

4. Giving instructions or asking someone to do something

Nimm bitte dein Biologiebuch heraus!

Ich?

Bringt bitte einen Atlas mit!

Wir?

Singular	bringe	.....	mit!
	nimm	.....	heraus!
	schlage	.....	auf!
	schreibe	.....	mit!
Plural	bringt	.....	mit!
	nehmt	.....	heraus!
	schlagt	.....	auf!
	schreibt	.....	mit!

Notice the different ending on the verb if you are speaking to more than one person.

G6

1. Describing people or things

Look at these examples:

> Meine Augen sind grün.
> Unsere Deutschlehrerin ist gut.

These words like *grün* and *gut* which describe people or things are called ADJECTIVES.

2. Saying what you like (doing)

> Schwimmen ist gut.
> Volleyball ist besser,
> aber am besten ist Fußball.

Notice how similar the German words here are to the English.

Now look at this:

> Thomas tanzt gut,
> Clive tanzt besser,
> aber Nadia tanzt am besten.

So you can use *gut, besser, am besten* after lots of different verbs, not just after *ist*.

Note: 1. The German word *gut* means both *good* and *well* in English.

2. In English where we have just one word (*best*), German needs two (*am besten*).

Now look at these examples:

Ich spiele gern Tennis.	*I like (playing) tennis.*
Conny spielt lieber Badminton.	*Conny prefers (playing) badminton.*
Matt spielt am liebsten Golf.	*Best of all Matt likes (playing) golf.*

So in German when you want to say what you like (doing), you use a verb (here *spielen*) plus *gern, lieber* or *am liebsten*.

If you want to say you like a person, you use *haben* or *mögen* plus *gern/lieber/am liebsten*.

Ich	habe / mag	meine Schwester gern.
Ich	habe / mag	meine Mutter lieber.
Am liebsten	habe / mag	ich meine Freundin Elisabeth.

3. Saying what you are interested in

Ich	interessiere	mich	für	Briefmarken.
Du	interessierst	dich	für	Fußball.
Er	interessiert	sich	für	Judo.
Sie	interessiert	sich	für	Reiten.
Wir	interessieren	uns	für	Rudern.
Ihr	interessiert	euch	für	Boxen.
Sie	interessieren	sich	für	Hockey.

Take a good look at all the parts of this verb (*Ich interessiere mich für ...*) – it is more complicated than other verbs you've met so far. It has an extra word (*mich, dich,* etc.) followed by *für*.

4. Saying "his", "her" and "their" in German

Das ist ihre Gitarre.
(her)

Das ist seine Gitarre.
(his)

Das ist ihre Gitarre.
(their)

Note: 1. The German for *his* is *sein(e)*.

2. In German, *ihr(e)* can mean *her* or *their*. Watch out for this.

1. Pronouns in the accusative

a)

Remember from Chapter 4 examples like *Ich habe einen Kuli*? Now look at this:

> Jutta, wie lange kennst du deinen Freund Michael? – Ich kenne ihn seit Jahren.
>
> Jutta, hast du das Training gern?   – Ja, ich habe es sehr gern.
>
> Jutta, wann siehst du die Clique?   – Ich sehe sie oft bei mir zu Hause.
>
> Jutta, magst du deine Eltern?   – Ja, ich mag sie sehr gern.

So you see that if you want to use a word (a pronoun) instead of *deinen* Freund you use *ihn*, and instead of *das Training* you use *es*, and so on.

Look carefully at these examples:

> Mein Fußball ist weg!   Wo ist er?
> Mein Fußball ist weg!   Ich finde ihn nicht!
> Wo ist meine Gitarre?   Siehst du sie?
> Magst du mein Modell?   Ich mag es nicht.

Note: The English word *it* can be *er, ihn, es* or *sie* in German.

b) "I/me/you"

Look at these examples:

> o Magst du mich nicht?
> ● Doch, ich mag dich sehr!

It's easiest if you remember:

> ich → mich
> du → dich

2. Question words

In German, many of these are easy, just like in English:

> Wann gehen wir?   *When ...?*
> Wie oft gehst du hin?   *How often ...?*
> Wie lange bleibst du da?   *How long ...?*

Note: German has two main ways of asking the time:

> Wie spät ist es?
> Wieviel Uhr ist es?

1. "Nach"/"zu" (= to)

In German there are two main ways of saying 'to' places:

a) with <u>named</u> countries and villages/towns ⟶ *nach*

> Ich fahre nach Deutschland.
> Sie fährt nach Kanada.
> Er fährt nach Berlin.

b) in almost every other case ⟶ *zu*

> Ich gehe zum Bahnhof.   (der Bahnhof)
> Wir fahren zur Schule.   (die Schule)
> Kommst du mit zum Schwimmbad? (das Schwimmbad)

> zum = zu dem
> zur = zu der

2. "An", "auf", "bei", "in", "neben"

Apart from *zu* and *nach*, there are other important words for saying exactly where something is:

> an   = *at, by*
> auf   = *on, at*
> bei   = *near, at (the house of)*
> in   = *in*
> neben = *beside, near*

These little words telling us <u>where</u> things are, are called PREPOSITIONS.

Look at these examples:

> Er wohnt in der Ringstraße.   (die Ringstraße)
> Sie steht neben dem Haus.   (das Haus)
> Die Katze sitzt auf dem Stuhl. (der Stuhl)

Notice in particular:

> Ich arbeite samstags im Kaufhaus. (das Kaufhaus)
> Die Disko ist am Rathausplatz.   (der Rathausplatz)
> Die Post ist beim Bahnhof.   (der Bahnhof)

> im   = in dem
> am   = an dem
> beim = bei dem

3. More about numbers

Remember the numbers you learned back in Chapter 3? Here are some other uses you can put them to:

eins	der/die/das erste	am ersten	Januar
zwei	zweite	zweiten	Februar
drei	dritte	dritten	März
vier	vierte	vierten	April
fünf	fünfte	fünften	Mai
sechs	sechste	sechsten	Juni
sieben	siebente	siebenten	Juli
acht	achte	achten	August
.....			
sechzehn	sechzehnte	sechzehnten	September
siebzehn	siebzehnte	siebzehnten	Oktober
.....			
zwanzig	zwanzigste	zwanzigsten	November
einundzwanzig	einundzwanzigste	einundzwanzigsten	Dezember
dreißig	dreißigste	dreißigsten	
vierzig	vierzigste	vierzigsten	

For example: Nehmen Sie die dritte Straße links!
Am ersten April fahren wir los.

G9

Some important verbs

There are five very important verbs in German which you use when you want to say what you want to do, what you can or can't do, what you're allowed or not allowed to do, etc. Look at these examples:

Ich will nicht zur Schule gehen.	*I don't want ...*
Du darfst jetzt gehen.	*You can (are allowed to) ...*
Hier darfst du nicht rauchen.	*You are not allowed to ...*
Kannst du gut Fußball spielen?	*Can you ...*
Er soll um 8 Uhr da sein.	*He is (supposed) to ...*
Ich muß meine Hausaufgaben machen.	*I have to ...*
Ich muß das nicht tun.	*I don't have to ...*

Note: 1. *ich darf nicht* means *I'm not allowed to, I must not;*
ich muß nicht means *I don't have to.*

2. After all these verbs, all the verbs in the infinitive (*gehen, spielen,* etc.) go to the END of the sentence.

See Lehrbuch, p. 82, for all the forms of these verbs, and for more examples.

Wie gut kannst du Deutsch?

1. Was ist das hier?

  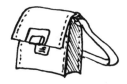 

ein / eine _____ _____ _____ _____

der / die / das _____ _____ _____ _____

2. Was tut Rocky gern?

_____ _____ _____ _____

_____ _____ _____ _____

3. Was sagen diese Leute?

_____ _____

_____ _____

_____ _____ _____

_____ _____ _____

Quellennachweis für Texte und Abbildungen

Heinrich Bauer Vertriebs KG, Hamburg (S. 94 o.) aus: "Fernsehwoche" 30/38

Bildarchiv Huber, Garmisch-Partenkirchen (S. 42)

Deutsche Bundesbahn (S. 88) aus: "Ihr Zugbegleiter", April 1983; (107) Skizze aus "Taschenfahrplan Oberbayern", 1982/83; (116) Fahrplanauszug

Deutscher Sportbund, Frankfurt/Main (Hg.) (S. 80, 83) aus: Heft 21 "Aktion Trimm Dich"

FISA I. G., Palaudarias, 26 Barcelona (S. 41) Ansichtskarte

Frankfurter Societäts-Druckerei GmbH, Frankfurt am Main (S. 83, 84) Fotos aus: "Scala-Jugendmagazin" 2/82; (89, 90) aus Sonderheft 2/81; (100) Text aus: Heft 1/81

Fremdenverkehrsamt München (S. 91) Adressen aus: "München-Leitfaden für Jugendgruppen", 1982

Bjarne Geiges (S. 9, 25 u., 64 o. + u., 67 r., 119, 124) Fotos

Goethe-Institut, München (S. 94, 104) Anzeigen aus: W. Lohfert "Schule und Freizeit, Texte zur Landeskunde", 1982

Kreisjugendring München-Land (Hg.) (S. 5, 48, 98, 99) aus: Prospekt "Burg Schwaneck", 1978, Redaktion Helmuth Mayr, Pullach/Isartal

Volker Leitzbach (S. 10/11, 12, 13, 17, 18, 21, 25 o., 29, 34, 49, 63, 64 Mi., 67 l., 75, 81, 85, 89, 90, 105) Fotos

Fritz Mader (S. 127) Foto

Otto Versand, Hamburg (S. 30, 31) Ausrisse aus Katalog

Polyglott Verlag, München (S. 14, 97, 121) Kartenskizzen

Theo Scherling (S. 7, 38) Collagen

Statistisches Bundesamt, Wiesbaden (Hg.) (S. 127) Kartenskizze aus: "Zahlenkompaß", 1982, Verlag W. Kohlhammer

Süddeutscher Verlag, München (S. 84) Tabelle aus: "Abendzeitung", München

Angelika Sulzer (S. 36, 37, 61, 62, 68, 110) Fotos

Velber Verlag, Seelze (S. 77, 79, 91) Leserbriefe und Zeichnungen aus: "Treff" Schülermagazin, 1978; (113) Zeichnung "Hausaufgaben" aus Heft 2/83; (123) Text aus: Heft 9/82

Verlag Deutsches Jugendherbergswerk, Hauptverband für Jugendwandern und Jugendherbergen e. V., Detmold (S. 48) Auszug aus: "Deutsches Jugendherbergsverzeichnis 1983/84"

WEREK Pressebildagentur, München (S. 14, 15) Fotos